Collection of Mr. Franklin Williams, Houston

FOLLOWING
GENERAL SAM HOUSTON

FROM
1793 to 1863

&

Etchings
by
Bernhardt Wall
Limerock, Connecticut

&

Historical Sketches
by
Amelia Williams, Ph. D.,
Austin, Texas

&

THE STECK COMPANY, *Publishers*
AUSTIN, TEXAS

PREFACE

The idea of collecting pictures by the means of which a brief life story of General Sam Houston might be traced from 1793, the year of his birth, to 1863, the year of his death, belongs solely to Mr. Bernhardt Wall, a well-known artist who claims Texas as the home of his adoption. Mr. Wall spent much time, and spared no pains, in collecting authentic pictures through which he might depict Houston's career; then, with his own inimitable skill he made etchings of these pictures. We heard of this unique plan, and were fortunate enough to secure the privilege of using his etchings. After much thought and discussion we decided to put the pictures into the hands of someone who could write brief historical sketches about them, and we chose Dr. Amelia Williams of Austin, Texas, for the task. Dr. Williams has an intimate knowledge of Texas history during the heroic period of the revolution, and for several years she has been engaged in compiling and preparing for publication an exhaustive collection of Houston's writings. Our instructions to her were to write sketches concerning the life of Houston that might be suggested by the pictures, each sketch to be within itself a complete story that might be used as a brief chapter of a book. Following this plan as mapped out for her, Miss Williams has made no pretension of writing a complete or logically connected biography of General Houston, but she has been careful never to state as an historical fact any detail that cannot be amply documented by Sam Houston's own writings, or by other reliable sources. Whenever it was possible, she has arranged the etchings and her sketches according to chronological sequence.

The Publishers.

Austin, Texas, 1935.

TABLE OF CONTENTS

(v)

Table of Contents, Cont'd

HOUSTOUN CASTLE JOHNSTONE, SCOTLAND
Collection of Mrs. Madge Hearne, Houston.

IN TIME

Houston

Collection of Mrs. Robt A. John, Houston.

The Houston Castle and Coat of Arms

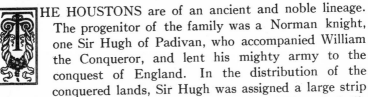HE HOUSTONS are of an ancient and noble lineage. The progenitor of the family was a Norman knight, one Sir Hugh of Padivan, who accompanied William the Conqueror, and lent his mighty army to the conquest of England. In the distribution of the conquered lands, Sir Hugh was assigned a large strip of territory that lay along the Scottish border. There he built his stronghold, but in a few years he became enfiefed to Malcolm, king of Scotland, who was the stepson of the ambitious but ill-fated Macbeth. The records tell that on one occasion when the King of the Scots and his army were hard pressed by their foes, Sir Hugh, at the head of fifty retainers, came to the rescue and bodily lifted his liege lord from the clutches of the enemy and bore him away to safety. For this timely succor the grateful king bestowed upon his rescuer the rank of a Scottish knight, and granted to him a rich estate in Renfrewshire. At the king's command, Sir Hugh's Norman coat-of-arms, which bore the device of ravens on a rectangular escutcheon, was changed by the addition of rampant greyhounds on either side of the shield, with a winged hour glass, in which the sands were almost run; above it, and surmounting the whole, ran a ribbon in graceful folds bearing the motto "In Tempore." These additions to the Norman symbols were to commemorate the swiftness with which Sir Hugh had brought assistance to his lord, just "in time," before the sands in the hourglass of Malcolm's life had run their course.

Sir Hugh married a highland chieftain's daughter and identified himself with the Scots; but as the simple Scotch people could never train their tongues to speak their lord's cognomen, Padivan, they contented themselves with calling him "Sir Hugh," and his castled estate *Hughstown*. As the generations passed, the descendants of this doughty knight came to be known as, and even to sign their own name, *Houston*.

The Houston line ran strong and true for several centuries, the majority of the men of the clan being noteworthy for their large, strong bodies and their intrepid fighting spirit. In the late seventeenth century, a man of the line, one Sir John Houston, restored much of the old baronial estate of the family. He reared a substantial castle, near Johnstone, Scotland, and became famed for his many brave deeds. Although his castle has long since passed away, pictures of it remain unto this day.

Sam Houston was born at Timber Ridge, near
Lexington, Virginia, March 2, 1793. This monument was erected by the Kiwanis Clubs of Lexington and Houston, near the site of the old home.

Collection of Mr Franklin Williams, Houston.

THE SITE OF SAM HOUSTON'S BIRTHPLACE, TIMBER RIDGE, NEAR LEXINGTON, VIRGINIA

N 1730, one John Houston, Gentleman, a descendant of Sir John Houston of Johnstone, Scotland, migrated to America and settled in Pennsylvania, near Philadelphia. Although he stayed there long enough to marry off his eldest son and two of his daughters, he never felt really satisfied among his German neighbors; so he decided to move to the Upper Valley of Virginia, where there was a settlement of his old Scotch friends, the Stuarts, the Paxtons, the McCorkles, the Davidsons, the McCormicks, and others. There he was happy, and there, by his shrewd Scotch sense and economy, he became one of the largest land owners, as well as one of the most influential citizens, of that famous old Presbyterian neighborhood. After his death his son Robert carried on the Houston tradition for independence of thought and civic usefulness. Robert settled on Timber Ridge plantation, seven miles from the little village of Lexington. He sent his son Samuel to join Washington's troops in the fight for American independence. The young man became infatuated with military service and was never able to enjoy the quiet of plantation life as did his kindred all about him; nevertheless, at his father's death, he inherited the Timber Ridge place, married Elizabeth, the daughter and heiress of old Squire John Paxton, the richest man of Rockbridge county, and tried to settle down. Elizabeth, tall and handsome, was counted every inch a lady, and a worthy mistress for Timber Ridge. She bore her husband nine children, Paxton, Robert, James, John, Samuel, William, Isabella, Mary, and Eliza Ann. The fifth son, Samuel, named for his father, was born at Timber Ridge, March 2, 1793; and it is with him that our stories will be chiefly concerned.

The numerous children of Major Samuel Houston were happy and full of youthful merriment. They had many kindred by the Houston name in the country round about Timber Ridge, and they always loved to visit their Cousin Matthew Houston, who lived in a fine house near High Bridge, the same that we know today as the Natural Bridge. But Major

Houston was never content as a planter, and he soon left the management of Timber Ridge to an overseer while he, as brigadier inspector of the state militia, went the rounds of a military career. A plantation needs the master's presence; so it happened that misfortunes and careless stewardship brought heavy losses to the Houston home, and, in 1806, Timber Ridge had to be sold for debt. Soon afterwards, Major Samuel Houston died; and in the spring of 1807, Elizabeth Paxton Houston, with her nine children and her household goods loaded on two large wagons drawn by nine fine horses, set out to make her home in Blount county, Tennessee. There her husband had traded for wild lands a short time before his death, and there she hoped to rear her children, and to retrieve, to some extent, at least, her lost fortune.

In their new home the family pioneered and prospered. Romance and adventure thrilled the children in this wilderness filled with wild beasts, birds, and Indians. The Indians became young Sam's especial diversion. He would sneak away from home and school to spend weeks, even months, among the Cherokees, whose nation lay not ten miles away from his mother's door. They received him as one of their own blood and taught him much of their cunning and much of their wisdom. In return, throughout his long life he continued to manifest a sincere concern for their welfare and for their future. Even when he sat as a senator in the Congress of the United States, speaking of himself in the third person, a habit acquired from the Indians, he declared: "Houston has seen nearly all there is in life to live for, and yet, he has been heard to say that when he looks back over the waste of years, there is nothing half so sweet to remember as this sojourn he made among the untutored children of the forest."

School-house, five miles from Maryville, Tenn., where Sam
Houston taught school, circa 1810-1813.
Collection, W. E. Parham, Maryville

The School House in Which Sam Houston Held School

AM HOUSTON never liked the restraint of the school-room. Even as a small boy, he escaped at every opportunity from the village school at Lexington; and he liked school no better in Tennessee than he had in Virginia. But while his dislike for the schoolroom was strong, he hated the routine of farm life, and that of the country store in which his older brothers set him to work. It was this distaste for routine work that sent him adventuring among the Indians. The consequence of it all was that the lad's schooling was very rudimentary. It is said, however, that he read every book that came his way. He himself has said that his ambition as a boy was to learn the *Iliad* in the original Greek; barred from that pleasure, on account of the lack of learned teachers, he did the next best thing: he practically memorized Pope's translation of the epic as he wandered among his Indian associates.

At the age of eighteen Houston found himself in debt, and, strangely enough, he chose to lift this burden by teaching school. In this decision, as in every other act of his life, he was original and daring. Five miles from Maryville, the little town near which his mother lived, there was a small log house— the same little hut that is pointed out to tourists today as Sam Houston's schoolhouse—in which the district school was taught for three or four months of each year. It was in this house that Houston opened his school. Theretofore, the school-masters of the district had charged only six dollars tuition per pupil for the entire term; Sam Houston announced that he would charge eight dollars per pupil, one-third of which must be paid in grain, one-third in red flowered calico, and one-third in money. To the surprise of his friends, he had a full school. At the end of three months he had paid off his debts, and he had an abundance of grain both for his own, and for his horse's food, and enough red calico to supply him with shirts for a whole year, with plenty left over for gifts for all the Indian maidens.

In later years an old comrade of the Indian wars once asked Houston which of the many honors that had come to him in life had given the greatest satisfaction: the presidency of the Republic of Texas; the position of commander-in-chief of the Texas army; or membership in the United States Senate. Without a moment's hesitation he replied: "When a young man in Tennessee, I once kept a country school. At the time I was about eighteen years old, and a tall and strapping fellow. At the noon hour, after the luncheon which I and my pupils ate together out of our baskets, armed with a well-trimmed hickory cane, dressed in a hunting shirt of flowered calico, my hair in a long queue down my back, with the sense of complete authority over my pupils, I experienced a higher feeling of dignity and self satisfaction than from any other office, or honor which I have since held."

Ensign Sam Houston in the Spring of 1814,
fighting at Horseshoe Bend, Alabama, being
severely wounded by bullets and an arrow.
From "Sam Houston and His Republic" 1846.

I N 1813 young Sam Houston reached his majority; he was ready for a man's life, and events were shaping themselves to that end. The War of 1812 had dragged drearily on for more than a year—mostly on the sea—when a recruiting detail settled down in Maryville for a period of duty. The call of centuries of fighting blood, the Houston love for military prowess and glory, burned strong in the young man's soul, and he determined to enlist for service against the British. Friends and relatives tried to dissuade him from going into the service as an enlisted man, but his mind was set. Through the influence of friends, however, it was not long before he received a commission as an ensign.

But Houston was destined never to see a British Redcoat. Instead, under General Andrew Jackson, he fought Creek Indians on the Tallapoosa river in Alabama, and at the battle of Tohopeka (Horse Shoe Bend) he was severely wounded. A barbed arrow stuck deep in his thigh, but still he led the men who had followed him into the thickest of the fight, and drove the Indians back from the palisade that protected the right wing of Jackson's men. As the fighting paused for a moment, Houston called upon the lieutenant of the company to pull the arrow out. Two attempts failed; the arrow was too deeply embedded in the flesh. Drawing his sword back over his head, Houston ordered his friend to try again, saying that he would cut him down if he failed. This time the lieutenant pulled out the arrow, leaving a jagged and gaping wound from which the blood gushed in a stream. While Houston was under the surgeon's hands, Jackson came up on horseback and ordered the boy to the rear, but Houston made light of his wounds and begged to be allowed to go back into the battle. This request Jackson sternly refused to grant, but when the General had ridden away, Houston disobeyed his order, recrossed the breastworks, and entered the battle again.

At the very crisis of the battle, Jackson called for volunteers to storm a ravine, but the hazard was so desperate that there was no response to the order. After a moment, however,

Houston dashed forward, calling upon his men to follow him, but he never looked back to see if they did so. Within a few feet of the entrance to the ravine, he received two bullets in his shoulder, and his upper right arm was shattered. His musket fell from his hand, and he was helpless. Then, for the first time, he saw that none of his men had supported his charge.

His wounds kept the young man under a doctor's care for more than a year; in fact, the shoulder wound was never perfectly healed, and it gave him trouble as long as he lived. His fearless bearing, however, gained for him the attention and admiration of General Jackson. A friendship and confidence developed between the two men that formed the most treasured relationship of Houston's life.

SAM HOUSTON
IN CHEROKEE INDIAN COSTUME
From a Miniature

Houston in Cherokee Indian Dress

AFTER the battle of Horse Shoe Bend, Houston's wounds were a long time in healing. As soon, however, "as he was able to walk straight and wear a uniform," he reported for service. He was given a commission in the regular army of the United States, and was assigned to duty in New Orleans. But his wounds continued to give trouble; because they failed to heal properly, he was compelled to solicit a transfer.

Through the influence of Houston's old friend, Governor McMinn of Tennessee, the President of the United States appointed Houston sub-agent to the Cherokees. This was a real advancement. Both Governor McMinn and the President had a double purpose in making the appointment: they hoped that the outdoor life among the Indians would benefit the young man's health; but, more especially, they hoped that Houston's knowledge of the character and customs of the Indians, as well as his sincere concern for their welfare, would help to overcome the reluctance of the Cherokees in the matter of their removal west of the Mississippi river. As the government officials had hoped, Houston soon persuaded the chiefs of the tribe that, in view of existing conditions, it would be to the advantage of the Cherokees to acquiesce in the plans of the government. In order to perfect the agreement of the head chiefs to the removal of their tribe, it was necessary for an Indian delegation to go to Washington to sign a treaty that would make the consent binding. Ever since Houston had been a sub-agent to the Cherokees, he had worked with the Indians as one of their own tribe. When, therefore, the delegation was ordered to Washington, he was numbered as one of the commission, and to please the Indians he wore the Cherokee dress.

At this time John C. Calhoun was the Secretary of War. He was a great stickler for military etiquette, and he sternly reprimanded Houston for appearing before him in Indian dress. It must be remembered that Houston was still an officer in the United States army, and military rules required that, while on duty, an officer must wear uniform. Moreover, Calhoun accused the young man of complicity with slave smugglers who were operating in the Indian territory; but Houston was able to make such emphatic denial of this charge, and to give such valuable information concerning the real wrongdoers, that even Calhoun was impressed with his story, and, at Houston's demand, allowed an investigation of the charges. Houston easily proved his own innocence; he also proved that he had been of great service to the government in checking the illicit trade. The case was dismissed, but the government did not even thank Houston for the services he had rendered, whereupon, feeling himself deeply aggrieved, he curtly resigned his commission in the United States army.

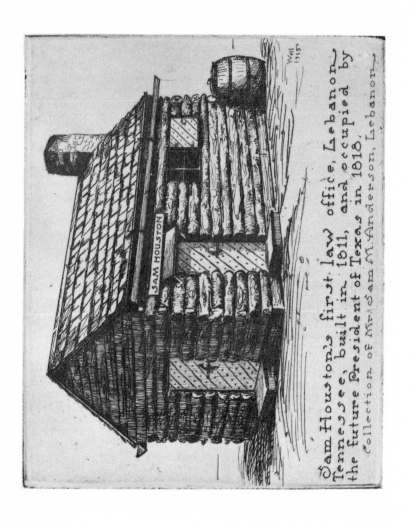

Sam Houston's first law office, Lebanon Tennessee, built in 1811, and occupied by the future President of Texas in 1818.
Collection of Mr. Sam M. Anderson, Lebanon

SAM HOUSTON

HOUSTON'S FIRST LAW OFFICE

HAVING put off his uniform and all the dignities that went with it, Houston became a private citizen and turned his attention to civil pursuits. But he had an enviable background of gallant military service, and he carried noble scars, silent testimony of his valor. Almost destitute of funds, he decided to study law. He made arrangement for a term of eighteen months of tutelage, and took up his studies in the law office of Judge James Trimble at Nashville; but impatient, impetuous Houston, after six months of intense study, passed an examination that gave him a license to practice law and admitted him to the Nashville bar. He decided, however, to locate for practice in the little town of Lebanon, of which Isaac Galliday was the postmaster and the town merchant.

Galliday liked the poor but brilliant young lawyer so well that he took him to live in his own home and provided an office for him. This office was a log hut, but it was stout and well built; in fact, it was far more comfortable and better situated than many other work shops that Houston was to occupy in higher positions during his later life. Galliday also credited him for the postage he used, which was no small item, for in 1818 it cost twenty-five cents to send a letter through the mails. Another important service that this kind benefactor rendered the young barrister was to fit him out with new clothes. For Houston this bit of generosity was probably the greatest service of all, for in everyday life he was always a great actor, and he never felt safe or secure in his performance unless he was properly dressed for the part as he had visualized it in his own mind.

During his life at Lebanon he made frequent trips to Nashville and usually stopped off at "The Hermitage" on the way. These visits kept him in touch with the prominent men of the state, and gave him the reputation of being himself a man of importance. On one of these visits he met Governor McMinn and returned to Lebanon with an appointment as adjutant-general of the state militia, with the rank of colonel. This office involved a good deal of tedious business that compelled the

young lawyer to make many tiresome journeys to Murfreesboro, the capital of the state, but on his return to his office
from one of them, he carried in his pocket his nomination as
attorney-general (prosecuting attorney) of the Nashville district. His election to that office necessitated his removal from
Lebanon.

This young man had made many friends in Lebanon. Although they were proud that one of the town's citizens had
achieved such success and honor, they were sad at his departure.
The whole town turned out to bid him farewell. Houston,
standing on the steps of the little courthouse, made an eloquent
speech, saying how much his life among them had meant to
him, and promising never to forget the friends at Lebanon.
His work in the new position as attorney-general was a success,
but after a year of service, he resigned to set himself up in private
practice at Nashville.

In every step of Houston's rising career we may clearly trace
the influence of his friend, Andrew Jackson, who himself was
becoming a figure of importance in national politics. Jackson's
admiration and love for his protégé grew stronger as the young
man manifested developing abilities, and in any matter that
closely concerned his interests, he began to rely on Houston's
loyal support. Jackson's friendship became Houston's most
treasured talisman.

Andrew Jackson, President of the United
States, 1829~1837, who was the great
friend and mentor of Sam Houston.
Collection of Mrs. I. D. McFarland, Houston

JACKSON'S PICTURE

HE career of Andrew Jackson is so familiar to all Americans that an attempt to write a biography of the man in connection with this picture would be presumptuous, certainly out of harmony with the purposes of this little book; nevertheless, it does seem fitting to make a few statements concerning the man who throughout life was Sam Houston's best friend.

Andrew Jackson (March 15, 1767—June 8, 1845) was born in South Carolina. At the age of thirteen he volunteered and served in the American Revolutionary army. In 1781 he was captured by the British, and was forced to suffer the most brutal treatment before he was released from his tortures by a general exchange of prisoners. Although his early education had been of the most rudimentary nature, he was admitted to the bar at Salisbury, North Carolina. In 1788, he opened a law office at Nashville, Tennessee, and ten years later he was appointed to a seat on the Supreme Bench of that state. At the beginning of the War of 1812, he offered his services to the Federal Government, and he was sent in 1813-1814 to fight the Creeks in Alabama. On January 8, 1815, he fought and won the battle of New Orleans, a victory that made him a national hero. He served as governor of Florida in 1821 and became a United States senator from Tennessee in 1823. Five years later he was elected the seventh President of the United States, and he was re-elected to that office in 1832. Many changes occurred during the eight years of his administration; some were wrought by Jackson's policies and his personal magnetism, but far more occurred as the result of an ever increasing development of industrial and economic interests within an agricultural nation. There are various points of view from which the man, the soldier, the President, may be studied; all are interesting. Opinions concerning the man are as varied; but right or wrong, strong or weak, Andrew Jackson is one of the most vital, one of the most interesting, of the men who have been President of the United States.

Such was the man whom fate gave to Houston for a friend. Throughout the vicissitudes of Houston's life Jackson never lost contact with his favorite, while Houston ever rendered to Jackson the reverential love of an only son for a devoted father. He was always happiest when he could feel that he honestly deserved as well as possessed his great patron's confidence.

The Hermitage, the home of Andrew Jackson near Nashville, Tennessee, where Sam Houston always was a welcome visitor.

Collection of Hon. T. H. McGregor, Austin

THE HERMITAGE—JACKSON'S HOME

ANDREW JACKSON named his plantation home *The Hermitage*. It was built in 1819, nine miles from Nashville on the Lebanon road. There Lafayette was royally entertained when he returned to America for a visit in 1824, and there the great, the near great, and the poor of the nation found hearty welcome for more than twenty years. The Hermitage was for Sam Houston a sanctuary, a haven to which he often went for pleasure, for counsel, and for consolation in times of doubt or misfortune. Its doors were always wide open to him, for he was a favorite not only with the master but with the mistress as well; she petted and scolded him by turns, calling him "my boy" or "you naughty fellow." In turn, Houston was truly fond of Mrs. Jackson. In the privacy of the home circle he usually called her "Aunt Rachel"; sometimes when he wished to wheedle her into good humor after some of his escapades, he would whisper softly, "my beautiful Mother Rachel." In the presence of strangers, however, or on state occasions, he would bend low over the lady's fat white hand with the formal "Madam," or "Lady Jackson." Trust Sam Houston for charms and graces with which to win the ladies!

This handsome old Southern homestead still stands, and all the furniture used by the Jacksons remains in the rooms just as it was while they lived. In addition there are now many glass cases in the house. These are filled with relics of the old master, while on the walls hang portraits of him, of his family, and of many of his friends. The office or library contains about four hundred and fifty books. In one of the glass cases in this room may be seen a picture of Houston, and in another there is a pair of Mexican hand-tooled leather leggings which Houston once presented to Jackson as a birthday gift. In fact, the house is now a veritable museum filled with mementos of those who once came and went within its old chambers. The kitchen, with all the pots and pans of the earlier day, is in splendid preservation, and close by are the smoke houses and the barns. Jackson's own carriages and other vehicles still stand in the old carriage house. Only a short distance beyond,

Uncle Alfred's cabin remains, a monument to the faithful old slave who loved and served his master's family throughout the ninety-eight years of his life, but whose highest earthly ambition was attained only in death, when his body was laid to rest close to that of his master in the garden of the old mansion.

The Capitol, Washington, D. C., where Congressman
Sam Houston of Tennessee, sat in sessions of
1823 — 1827

From Following Marquis de Lafayette, 1824

The Capitol of the United States as It Appeared When Sam Houston Served as a Representative From Tennessee

STILL mindful of our purpose to follow the steps of Houston's career, we return to our main theme. In 1823 he was elected a representative from Tennessee to the United States Congress. When he took his seat in that body, the capitol building presented a very different appearance from that of the present day. Neither the north nor the south wing had been constructed, and the building was topped by an unsightly wooden dome, from the height of which no statue of Liberty looked down upon the city below.

James Monroe was the President. Henry Clay, Daniel Webster, John Randolph of Roanoke, John Quincy Adams, John C. Calhoun, and Andrew Jackson were probably the most prominent men of the times. Jackson's friendship for Sam Houston was known afar, and it served the newly elected congressman as both introduction and passport into all the governmental circles, and gave him intimate association with many men of fame and power. When Lafayette returned to visit Washington in 1824, Houston was there, and the mutual love of these two men for Andrew Jackson and his wife drew the old French nobleman and the young representative from Tennessee into a close relationship. These two queerly matched friends met again under the hospitable roof of the Hermitage, where Lafayette related to the eagerly attentive Houston detailed accounts of his experiences in the French Revolution.

But Houston's pathway to political advancement was not all strewn with roses; nor was his intense loyalty to Jackson an unmixed blessing for him, for the "Old Chief" had strong enemies who were always glad to strike a blow at the master by offering slights to, and erecting handicaps in the way of, the coterie of young protégés whom he had drawn about him. In 1824 Jackson was one of four candidates for the presidency, and although he received the highest number of electoral votes, he did not get a majority; so the final decision of the election had

(41)

to go to the House of Representatives. There, by the so-called trade between Henry Clay and John Quincy Adams, Jackson lost the presidential chair, and when John Quincy Adams subsequently appointed Clay Secretary of State, the appointment caused great bitterness of feeling among the political factions. Out of this strife and hard feeling new party alignments developed; the Jacksonian party grew strong and well-defined, and as its main objective was to elect its leader to the presidency in 1828, an intensive campaign to that end was initiated and maintained. In fact, the four years of John Quincy Adams' administration are marked by political animosity and intrigue on the part of his opponents to prevent his re-election; but these various plots and combinations are too complex and too long-drawn-out to be related here.

During the last two years of Houston's service in the House he was very active in the interests of his beloved patron. In 1824, and again in 1828, John C. Calhoun was elected Vice President. And it may be remembered that John C. Calhoun was Houston's inveterate enemy. He never lost an opportunity to snub and slight the young man, and it became a bitter trial to Houston's impulsive, imperious nature, though probably a very valuable lesson in self-control, to bear silently and with smiling good humor the open slights and the frequent but veiled jibes of his old enemy. So, while to discerning persons it was clear that Houston and Calhoun were no better friends than of old, political exigency compelled the young congressman from Tennessee to treat the Vice President with courtesy and deference, for it was well known at Washington that Calhoun's alignment with the Jackson party had given it great strength; indeed, Calhoun's adherents openly bragged that it required Calhoun's wisdom to save the Jackson party from oblivion. The Tennessee contingency bore this taunt with ill-suppressed bitterness and gladly welcomed Martin Van Buren when he brought his following into their ranks. True, Van Buren had joined the Jacksonian party for selfish reasons, but he was as skillful a leader as Calhoun, and not half so self–assertive; so from the time of his advent into their ranks, he was in close association with the peculiarly Jackson group, and the party soon developed a faction within itself that was kept in bounds only by the necessity of meeting a common danger. Consequently, after the election of Jackson in 1828, this rift broadened and deepened; hard feelings sprang up between the President and the Vice President that grew into the bitterest enmity. One result of the spleen that Calhoun had always vented against Houston may be traced in the famous Calhoun-Jackson quarrel. For two years Houston held within his possession the letter that finally convinced Jackson that in 1818, when Calhoun was Secretary of War, he had wished to discipline Jackson for the invasion of Florida. As long as it would not promote Jackson's interests for this letter to be produced, Houston withheld it for fear the sudden anger that Jackson was sure to feel upon reading it might do his cause harm, but when it became evident that it would possibly break Calhoun for the document to see light, it was placed in the President's hands. The ultimate result was much as had been expected. Jackson turned all his influence to the interests of Van Buren as his successor. Thus, the long enmity between Calhoun and Houston probably played its part in preventing the great South Carolinian from reaching the goal of his life's ambition—the presidency.

But amid all the strife and turmoil of politics, Houston found many compensating joys during his membership in Congress. He was young, barely past his thirtieth birthday; he was the favorite of a powerful man, and seemed to have, in his own right, a secure future; moreover, he was handsome and possessed of many graces. Friendships came to him easily, and he was a welcome guest in whatsoever salon or household he chose to enter. Mounted on a well-chosen, fiery horse, he cut no mean figure, and his social excursions were extended to a wide radius about the capital city. Many interesting stories might be told of his social experiences, but only two can be related in this little book.

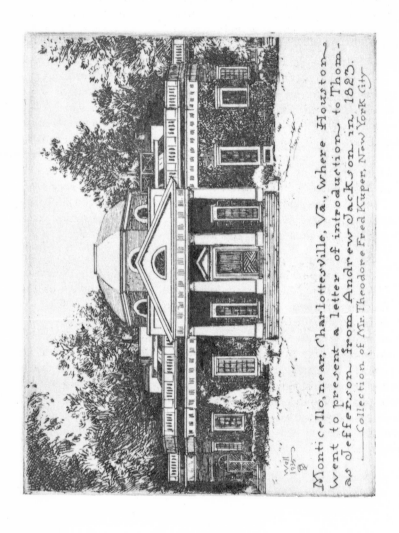

Monticello, near, Charlottesville, Va., where Houston went to present a letter of introduction to Thomas Jefferson from Andrew Jackson in 1823.

Collection of Mr. Theodore Fred Kuper, New York City

Monticello, the Home of Thomas Jefferson

WHEN Thomas Jefferson was Vice President in 1797 and presided over the Senate, he came to know bluff Andrew Jackson, the senator from the newly admitted state of Tennessee. But Jefferson's expressions concerning the parliamentary conduct of the Tennesseean were far from flattering, and even after twenty-seven years of military service that had made Jackson the idol of the nation, when he returned to the Senate as the hero of New Orleans and subsequently became a candidate for the presidency, he found that Jefferson had not changed his opinion. In fact, Jefferson fearlessly stated that Jackson was not fitted to become the President of the United States, because of his lack of knowledge of parliamentary procedure, and because of his inexperience in diplomatic relations. It is a well-known fact that Jefferson backed William H. Crawford for the presidency; but he was fated to see his favorite defeated, and Jackson as well, nor did he live to see the Jacksonian victory of 1828. But in spite of all this political difference Jackson and Jefferson were personal friends. Jefferson liked the man Jackson and praised him without stint as a military chieftain.

Now, Sam Houston was well aware of the difference in caste and opinion between Jefferson and his friend; still he had a curiosity and a somewhat reverent desire to meet the old sage of Monticello. Jackson willingly made this wish possible of fulfilment by giving Houston a letter of introduction to Jefferson, and it was through the medium of this letter that Houston was able to enjoy the pleasure of an entire day of conversation with the learned man, as well as a delightful visit in his beautiful mansion.

Arlington, Va., where Congressman Houston was
wont to visit Mary Parke Custis, later, Mrs. R.E. Lee.
Collection of Mrs. I. B. McFarland, Houston

Arlington, the Home of Mary Parke Custis

SOME of Houston's wanderings about the environs of Washington carried him on more sentimental excursions than his visit to Monticello. For a time he was a frequent visitor at beautiful, classic Arlington on the Potomac. There lived the charming Mary Parke Custis, the granddaughter of Washington's stepson, and the only surviving representative of the "Father of our Country." This young woman was the heir of historic Arlington and its landed estates. The story goes that Houston once entertained hopes of becoming the master of this old mansion; but his ambitions in that direction were "nipped in the bud," for the fair Mary frankly told him that she had long since given her heart and promised her hand to her childhood sweetheart, who was then a cadet at West Point. Houston's heart wound at this turn of affairs was probably not deep, although he is known to have confided to one friend that he was disappointed in "the good taste and discernment of Mary Custis who preferred to tie herself by a long engagement to that shy underclassman at West Point when she might have become Houston's bride and the belle of Washington society." About this same time he wrote to another friend: "I am making myself less frequent in the Lady world than I have been. I must keep up my dignity, or rather, I must attend more to politics and less to love . . . ."

But Destiny was driving Sam Houston's career hard and fast. Long ere Mary Custis became the bride of Second Lieutenant Robert Edward Lee, in 1831, Sam Houston had been stricken by the cruel darts of fate.

The Masonic Temple, Nashville, Tenn., the home of Cumberland Lodge, No. 8, F. & A. M., of which Gen. Sam Houston was a member. Here met the General Assembly during the administration of Governor Sam Houston, 1827-1829.

Courtesy of Mrs. John Trotwood Moore, Nashville.
Tennessee State Library

THE OLD MASONIC TEMPLE AT NASHVILLE, TENNESSEE

BEFORE Houston's term of office as United States congressman had expired in 1827, he had been elected governor of Tennessee. During the early days of its history as a state, the capital of Tennessee, like that of Texas, was located at various places—at Knoxville, Kingston, Murfreesboro, Nashville. With the beginning of Houston's gubernatorial term, however, the capital was permanently located at Nashville, but before an adequate state capitol could be built, the several departments of government were distributed among various buildings of the city. Thus it happened that while Houston was governor of Tennessee (1827-1829), the Legislature of the state held its sessions in the Masonic Hall. A resolution of the Legislature, December 15, 1827, testifies to this fact: "Resolved, that the thanks of this General Assembly be expressed to the owners of the Masonic Hall, for the use of the respective rooms in which our deliberations have been conducted, and that the Secretary of State ascertain the casual damage to the windows, shutters, etc., which has been done during the session in consequence of its use, and have the same repaired and present his act, to the next session of the General Assembly.

John H. Camp,
Speaker of the House of Representatives.

W. Hall,
Speaker of the Senate."

This Masonic Hall was also the meeting place of Cumberland Lodge No. 8, the lodge of which Houston was a member. Not many positive facts can be found concerning Houston's life as a Mason, but the following data may be of interest. The records of the Grand Lodge of Texas show that Samuel Houston received his Entered Apprentice degree in masonry in the Cumberland Lodge No. 8, of Nashville, Tennessee, April 19, 1817, that he was advanced to the Fellowcraft degree, June

(49)

20, 1817, and became a Master Mason on July 22, of the same year. He demitted from Cumberland Lodge No. 8, November 20, 1817. It is not known where he carried his membership, but it is probable that he remained unattached to any lodge for about three years. On June 21, 1821, he applied for re-admission to Cumberland Lodge No. 8 and was accepted; he then remained a member of that body until January 20, 1831, at which time he applied for and received another demit. For six years no record can be found concerning his masonic affiliation, other than tradition in the Milam Lodge No. 2 and the McFarland Lodge No. 3 (now Red Land Lodge No. 3), of Nacogdoches and San Augustine, respectively, that he was a frequent visitor in both these bodies. Why he remained un-affiliated we do not know.

On November 13, 1837, however, he applied for and received membership in Holland Lodge No. 36 (now Holland No. 1). He remained a member of this body until July 14, 1842, upon which date he asked for and received a demit. The records are not clear concerning other affiliations that he may have made in 1842, but the minutes of Forest Lodge No. 19 (Huntsville, Walker county) show that in 1851 he was a member of that body.

At the formation of the Grand Lodge of Texas on December 20, 1837, Houston was called to the chair as Worshipful Master, *pro tem.*, while Anson Jones was appointed Secretary, *pro tem.* As a result of this meeting, however, Houston held no office in the newly organized Grand Lodge; nevertheless, it may be of interest to enumerate the first elected officials of that body. They were: Anson Jones, Worshipful Master; Adolphus Sterne, District Deputy; Jefferson Wright, Senior Warden; Christopher Dart, Junior Warden; James H. Winchell, Secretary; Thomas G. Western, Treasurer.

Although Houston may have been a very active Mason, few references can be found to indicate the fact. But the Masonic Order does its work so secretly that the world seldom knows of its activities. There is, however, a tradition backed by fairly substantial evidence, which tells that Santa Anna owed his life at San Jacinto to the fact that he was a Mason, and that he gave the distress signs, first to James A. Sylvester, one of his captors, secondly, to Houston when he was brought before the General, and thirdly, to a group of Texan soldiers, among whom were John A. Wharton, George W. Hockley, Sidney Sherman, and others. These Masons are said to have worked together in order to save the Mexican general's life.

Nashville Inn, Nashville, Tennessee, where lived Sam Houston, when Governor. Here he brought his bride, Eliza Allen, in January, 1829.

Collection of the Carnegie Public Library, Nashville.

The Nashville Inn

N THE previous sketch it was stated that before Houston's term of office as United States congressman had expired, he was elected governor of Tennessee. His predecessor in this office was William Carroll, an astute, ambitious politician who had held the office for the three preceding terms, the constitutional limit of service that any one man could have in the office without an intervening term by another. Carroll claimed to be Houston's friend and had worked for his election; he had even tacitly, if not definitely, promised not to become a candidate for the office again until Houston had served two consecutive terms. But ambitious, unscrupulous politicians easily forget or wilfully renounce promises; so it was with Carroll. In the early days of 1829, he announced that he would be a candidate against Houston for the governor's office in the coming election. Carroll was rich, powerful, and popular; but as Houston was also popular and powerful, the race promised to be both exciting and close.

In the meantime, Houston had been married, January 22, 1829, to Eliza Allen, the belle of Sumner county. Her father's large estate lay along the Cumberland river, a little distance from the town of Gallatin. Naturally, this marriage had caused quite a social stir in Tennessee, especially in the fashionable circles of Nashville, where the brilliant young governor's bachelorhood had been a constant source of comment and speculation. When, therefore, his marriage was announced the tongues of society stood still in surprise, for the news had come unexpectedly. Soon, however, there was a wholehearted rally, and all the city was glad that the governor was to have his own household. The charming young bride was sincerely welcomed; and the old Nashville Inn—headquarters for all good Jacksonians—where Houston lived, and where he brought Eliza, took on new life and gayety.

But Houston had little time in which to enjoy his honeymoon, for as we know, he had set his heart on a second term as governor. The success of his election seemed a vital matter to him now, partly to satisfy his own ambitions, but mostly, no doubt, because he wished to give his young wife the proud distinction of ruling Nashville society as the "First Lady of Tennessee." The honeymoon had scarcely waned, therefore, before the bridegroom had to take the stump against his competitor for the occupancy of the governor's chair.

The first joint meeting of the contenders for the office was on April 16, 1829. Houston went into the campaign with eloquence and vim and was told by his scouts, who had secretly felt the pulse of public sentiment, that the day had been in his favor. He returned to Nashville and hastened with his good news to Eliza.

Court House, Gallatin, Tennessee, where were kept the records of marriage of Sam Houston and Eliza Allen

Collection of Mrs. Sarah Fitz Gerald Lee, Gallatin

The Court House at Gallatin, Tennessee

UT something had happened. Eliza had gone to the home of her parents and refused to return to her husband. Soon the news got out, and all the city was amazed and curious. But Houston sealed his lips; he refused to make any explanation to the curious world beyond saying that he exonerated Eliza fully. The Allens, likewise, refused to talk about the matter. No one knew anything about the causes of the tragedy, and we know hardly more today. But we do know that this unfortunate circumstance seemed to shake the very foundations of Houston's life. It altered his entire being and brought about monumental changes in the history and in the development of a nation.

After two days of hard and silent work in setting his official affairs in order, Houston wrote a letter to William Hall, Speaker of the State Senate and constitutional successor if, for any reason, the governor's office should become vacant, resigning the gubernatorial chair. In disguise, accompanied by only two friends, Houston left Nashville, ambition and desire behind him. Eliza secluded herself in her father's home, very probably to repent, at leisure, her hasty and childish act.

The Allen estate, with its beautiful colonial home, was completely ravished during the Civil War. Nothing remains today of this handsome Southern homestead to remind the sympathetic or the curious-minded of the scenes where Sam Houston and Eliza Allen lived and loved. Perhaps the old court house at Gallatin, where their marriage contract was recorded, is now the only building left standing that can bear witness that Sam Houston passed that way. Perhaps it could tell of a young man's high hopes, of his expanding ambitions, of his passionate love; but its old walls stand grim and silent.

From an Engraving in "Sam Houston and his Republic," 1846.
Wall 1925

Houston resigned as Governor of Tennessee, & lived with the Cherokees near Ft. Gibson, Ind.Ty. from April, 1829, until November, 1832.

Houston in the Dress of the Civilized Indian

WITH ambition defeated and home life shattered, Sam Houston put the white man's civilization behind him. He had always loved the Indians; many of the happiest days of his boyhood had been spent among them, and he had long ago been adopted as a fully privileged member of the Cherokee tribe. Now in the hour of his misfortune his mind turned again to his old friends. He decided to make his way to the Arkansas Territory where the Cherokees then lived. Upon his arrival the old head chief, Oo-loo-te-ka, ran out to meet him, and embraced him with affection, saying: "My son, my son! My wigwam is yours; my home is yours; my people are yours—rest with us." In after years Houston wrote of this occasion: "Houston has often been heard to say that when he laid himself down to sleep that night, he felt like a weary wanderer returned, at last, to his father's house."

The Indians prepared a great feast for him. They had rejoiced when they heard that he had become the chief of a great state; they rejoiced still more that he had returned to their crude lodgings, for life had not gone well for them in the West. They felt that Houston, whose friendship with the "Great White Father" at Washington was so well known, would serve them as a friend at court.

But after a few days of joyous freedom and rest, Houston was no longer his old active self. He dropped into a lethargy that seemed to rob him of all ambition, all desire ever again to live a white man's life in a white man's civilization. Round about Fort Gibson, near which the Indians had their lands, he was known as a drifter, as a man who seemed to have lost all sense of the passing of time. Once, however, when Washington Irving passed that way with a government commission, Houston bestirred himself and enjoyed a week of fishing with the company, but when the visitors had continued their journey, he dropped back into his old stupor.

After more than two years of listless drifting, a real grievance of his Indian friends aroused him, and he determined to go with them to Washington to see the President. Houston knew that he would find a welcome at Washington, for during all this time Jackson had never entirely lost touch with his former favorite. The news of the rupture of Houston's marriage had surprised and saddened the old man, for to him this misfortune was as much a mystery as it was to the rest of the world. Just before he had set out upon his journey to Washington in 1829, he had given the young couple his blessing and felt confident that they had before them a life of domestic happiness; then came the news of their separation and of Houston's flight into the wilderness.

Moreover, wild tales of a wilder scheme in which Houston was said to be implicated, reached the President's ears. It was to the effect that Houston, abetted by his Indian foster father, had on foot an imperialistic scheme of considerable magnitude, and one of possible danger to the friendly relations between the United States and Mexico. It was rumored that Houston was planning to conquer Texas—even all Mexico— and set up a great empire to the west of the Mississippi river with himself as its ruler. The Cherokee Indians, succored by a federation of the western tribes, were to be the military force to put into effect this dazzling project.

Now Washington was not ignorant of the fact that the Indians were dissatisfied with conditions in the territory to which they had been moved, nor that Oo-loo-te-ka, as the representative of several tribes, had dreamed of, and had made definite plans to effect, a federation of the western Indians, in order that a great Indian government might be set up in the West; consequently, Jackson took steps to investigate carefully the activities of his former protégé, and he also took measures to contravene him, if he should find the stories afloat to be true. All the while, however, his loyal old heart ached for his friend; so putting all other considerations aside, he wrote to the self-exiled man. After writing of the pain he felt at Houston's broken marriage and broken prospects he said: "Oh, how unstable are human affairs! What a reverse of fortune!" He then mentioned the rumors that he had heard and sought a pledge from Houston that they were untrue.

In reply Houston wrote from a sickbed, "Your letter was a cordial to my spirits. Had a scepter been dashed at my feet, it would not have afforded the same pleasure, which I derived from the proud consciousness, not only that I deserved, but that I *possessed your confidence!*" Indirectly, he promised that he would take no future steps without Jackson's knowledge and consent—"were I disposed to abandon my present seclusion, I would submit to you (concerning what would be) most advantageous." He frankly said, however: "It might so happen, were I settled in a state; that I might render my aid in some future struggle between usurpation, and the rights of the people, in wresting power from the hands of the corrupt Usurper." Rather a vague pledge, perhaps, that he would engage in no rash plans, but all Jackson's fears were allayed concerning Houston's loyalty and honorable intentions; hadn't he said he would submit to the President his plans if he should leave his seclusion? That was assurance enough for Jackson from Houston. It is little wonder, then, that Houston felt sure of a welcome and an interested hearing when he set out for Washington in December, 1831, with an Indian delegation who bore to the "Great White Father" a written recital of their grievances.

For this trip Houston decided that he would repeat his plans of earlier days. The Indians desired it, and he deemed it a dramatic appeal to popular sympathy; therefore, he went as a member of the delegation, dressed as a civilized Indian. Every chief of the various tribes represented by the delegation contributed to Houston's attire for the occasion, and five complete costumes made up his wardrobe of rich, handsomely beaded and colorful garments. The Creek chief had presented a buckskin coat incrusted with beads and silver ornaments that tinkled musically as its wearer walked; another chief had contributed a large felt hat, the wide brim of which was embroidered with beads and silver, while handsome eagle feathers waved from one side of the crown. But in spite of all this pagan richness of attire, Houston had not a single suit such as was worn by civilized white men, and he had no money with which to buy one.

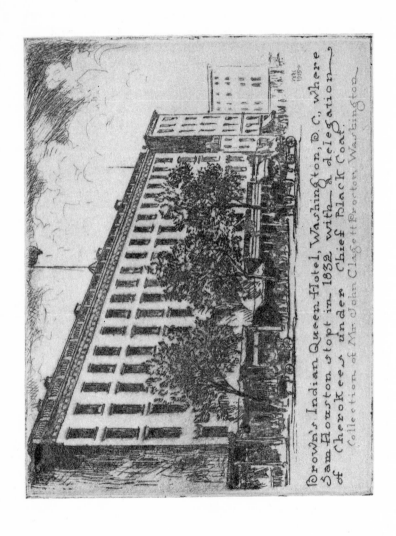

Brown's Indian Queen Hotel, Washington, D.C., where Sam Houston stopt in 1832 with a delegation of Cherokees under Chief Black Coat. Collection of Mr. John Clagett Proctor, Washington.

BROWN'S INDIAN QUEEN HOTEL

E N ROUTE to Washington the travellers stopped off at Nashville. They went out to the Hermitage, where Houston took pride in showing his Indian friends the private home of the "Great White Father." While strolling through the grounds Houston used, for the first time, a very handsome knife that one of the chiefs had given him as a parting gift. He cut a hickory sapling, and trimmed it for a walking cane. Upon their arrival in Washington, the delegation made their headquarters at Brown's Indian Queen Hotel on Pennsylvania Avenue, halfway between the Capitol and the White House. Houston felt very much at home in this hostelry, for he had lived there during the years that he had served as a congressman from Tennessee. He was destined to remain in this old familiar place for a much longer time than he dreamed when he signed his name on the register, along with the other members of the delegation.

It was on this trip to Washington that Houston got into an altercation with one William Stanbery, a member of Congress from Ohio. In the course of a broad criticism of Jackson's administration, Stanbery made caustic remarks about Houston and John Eaton (Secretary of War) in relation to contracts for furnishing Indian rations. He said: "Was not the late Secretary of War removed because of his attempt fraudulently to give Governor Houston the contract for Indian rations?" Houston sent the gentleman a note by Cave Johnson of Tennessee, which contained the formalities preceding a challenge to a duel. Stanbery ignored the challenge, saying that he declined to reply to a "note signed Sam Houston." Thereupon Houston declared that he would introduce himself to "the rascal." Hearing of this threat, Stanbery armed himself with two pistols, while Houston sought out the walking cane that he had cut from the grounds of the Hermitage. An opportunity for the ceremony of introduction soon came. Meeting Stanbery on the street late one evening, Houston asked: "Are you Mr. Stanbery?" Upon receiving an answer that he was, Houston fell upon the man and began beating him with the hickory cane. Stanbery tried to use his pistols, but they missed fire. The result was that Houston's cane and his boots were used to such effect that Stanbery had to take to his bed.

Naturally, the event created a great furore. Houston was arrested and arraigned before the House of Representatives, and one of the most spectacular trials ever held before that body continued for a whole month. Houston engaged Francis Scott Key as his attorney, but he virtually conducted his own case.

The White House, Washington, D.C., where Sam Houston was a frequent visitor while acting as Ambassador of the Cherokees in 1832

Collection of Mrs. Rutgers Fish, Lime Rock, Ct

The White House at Washington

ALL WASHINGTON knew that during the Houston-Stanbery trial and afterwards Sam Houston lived more at the White House than at Brown's Hotel, where he was registered. Jackson was greatly disturbed at one point in the trial when it seemed that Houston might have the affair go sadly against him. Much comment and a good deal of harsh criticism were floating about, engendered by the fact that Houston walked the streets in Indian dress; so one day Jackson tossed a long knitted silken pouch across the table to his favorite with the command, "Go dress like a gentleman." Houston did not need a second bidding, for nothing delighted him more than good clothes *a la mode*, and thenceforth he appeared everywhere dressed in the latest fashion.

The outcome of his case was a conviction, the punishment to be a "severe reprimand" at the hands of the Speaker of the House. The Speaker was one of Houston's best friends and had spent the night before the final day of the trial in Houston's hotel bedroom with other boon companions of equal fame and position. It is needless to say that Mr. Stevenson made a mere formality of his unwelcome duty, saying: "I pronounce the judgment of this House, which is that you be reprimanded at this bar by the Speaker, and . . . . I do reprimand you accordingly."

William Stanbery, whose name, but for this trial, would probably have died in oblivion, was not satisfied with the punishment meted out; so he had Houston arrested on the charge of criminal assault, and brought to trial in the civil courts. He was found guilty and fined $500, but before Jackson left the presidency he exerted his pardoning power to remit the fine. In after years as Houston reviewed the Stanbery case he said: "I was dying out. Had they taken me before a justice of peace and fined me ten dollars it would have killed me; but they gave me a national tribunal for a theatre, and that set me up again."

(67)

Jackson was delighted with the outcome of the matter. The intimacy of old times was restored between himself and his favorite. Houston was again one of his family; he was again a white man, and in the political harness; and he was destined for a new life, a new adventure, a new era both for himself and for his country.

Remains of Fort Towson on the Red River, Indian Territory. Houston left for Texas, early Dec. 1832
Collection of Grant Foreman, Esq., Muscogee.

FORT TOWSON

E MAY be sure that after Houston's trial was over, he and Jackson talked often and long concerning the future. What plans were made between them we do not know for certain, but logical conclusions may be drawn from subsequent events. Some of the facts in hand are: that from boyhood Houston had been deeply interested in the Indians, especially the Cherokees; that after his exile (1829) he had no doubt dreamed and planned with Oo-loo-te-ka for the conquest of Texas—even of Mexico—and for the establishment of the empire in the West; that Jackson had changed these plans with a letter, and the dream had vanished in a pledge that a young man gave to his friend and patron not to upset deep-laid diplomatic schemes for the purchase of the very land that he had thought to conquer. But Jackson's plans to buy Texas had failed of fruition time and again. Did he now in 1832 release Houston from the old pledge? Did he even plot with him concerning ways and means, more secure than Cherokee backing, for the taking of the coveted Texas? Who knows? Who will ever positively know? What we do positively know is that as Houston left Washington, Jackson gave him $500 and concocted a mission that would carry him to Texas under a United States passport.

After leaving Washington, Houston spent the next three months settling his private affairs at Fort Gibson, near which he had lived during his exile. This accomplished, he mounted his horse and swung southward, across the country, toward the land of cactus, scrub oaks, mesquites, and missions.

Arriving at old Fort Towson, then, as now, in ruins, he sat his horse and gazed across the river into Texas. An old friend, Elias Rector, of Arkansas, accompanied him to the river's brink, but could go no further. Before parting, perhaps forever, Rector wished to give his friend a present, but he had nothing suitable to offer except a fine razor. This he tendered. Houston accepted the gift, saying: "I accept your gift, and mark my words, Rector, if I have luck this razor will some day shave the chin of the president of a republic." Spurring his pony into the muddy stream (the Red river), Houston crossed his Rubicon and entered the land that for the next thirty-one years was to be verily his own country.

.

The Veremendi House, home of the Vice-Governor, in San Antonio, Texas, where Houston was introduced by Col. James Bowie, after Christmas, 1852.
Courtesy of Mr. Harry Hertzberg, a Friend, San Antonio

THE VERAMENDI HOUSE

AM HOUSTON first touched Texas soil on December 2, 1832. In later years his enemies sometimes taunted him and called him a coward, but his very advent into Texas is good proof of a brave spirit. It required courage and self-confidence to come all alone into a strange land that he knew was filled with hostile Indians, wild beasts, and indefinite trails.

The first settlement in which he stopped for any length of time was Nacogdoches on El Camino Real, near the Louisiana border. There he found friends of the old Tennessee days, an agreeable experience after the hardships of forest travel. He stayed there long enough to rest his weary horse, and then pressed onward over the King's Highway, deviating from the well-marked road in order to find the town of San Felipe de Austin, the capital of Stephen F. Austin's colony. The impresario was absent on a trip, but at this place Houston met Jim Bowie and ate Christmas dinner with him.

James Bowie was another American adventurer, a land speculator, who had made his way into Texas several years before this time from Louisiana. He had married Ursula de Veramendi, daughter of Juan Martin de Veramendi, who was the Vice-Governor of the dual state of Coahuila-Texas. Veramendi made his home at San Antonio de Bexar, a town that was indiscriminately called by the Texans San Antonio or Bexar. At Bexar, Veramendi was the leader of a group of intelligent Mexicans whose ancestors had settled the town while it was under Spanish rule. These San Antonio Mexicans were, for the most part, fairly well educated men of honor and integrity, who were proud of their race and its heritage, but who welcomed the coming of the American settlers as a means of developing their fair land. Had Mexico been able to settle Texas with this type of her native stock, our state would very probably remain today a state of the Mexican Republic. But Mexico was never able to induce her better class of citizens to colonize her northern territory, and it is a well-known fact that the few Mexican settlements that were made in Texas—usually around the presidios—were of the very lowest element of the Mexican people.

While they were eating their Christmas dinner, Houston told Bowie that San Antonio was his destination, and that he had a commission from the President of the United States to treat with the Comanche Indian chiefs concerning the matter of border depredations, whereupon Bowie invited him to be his guest while in San Antonio. The invitation was accepted and the men rode on together. Upon their arrival at San Antonio, Veramendi greeted the newcomer with a gracious welcome, and during his stay at Bexar, Houston was an honored guest in the Veramendi home.

Aided by Bowie and Veramendi, he was able to call together the Comanche chiefs with little delay. He spread out before them his official papers and held a general powwow. These interviews with the Indians were long and earnest, but Houston never explained their nature or their substance, except to say that they were "confidential matters between himself and Jackson," and that the ends "contemplated" had been "accomplished."

Having finished his business in San Antonio, Houston retraced his steps along the King's Highway to San Felipe. This time he found Austin at home, and enjoyed long talks with him. At San Felipe he also met his old-time friends, William H. and John A. Wharton, men whom he had known as boys, in happier days, at Nashville, Tennessee. Since they had first heard of his exile from civilization, these brothers had been writing to him to join them in Texas. William H. Wharton had recently married the daughter of Jared Groce, the richest man in the Texas colonies, while John A. was already making for himself a fine reputation in his law practice. These men used their best arguments to induce Houston to remain in Texas, but he was eager to press on to complete his mission.

Old Stone Fort, Nacogdoches, Texas. In Nacogdoches, in 1833, Sam Houston became
a practicing attorney.
Collection of KirKaid School, Houston

The Old Stone Fort at Nacogdoches

OUSTON did not stop long to rest until he had reached Natchitoches, Louisiana, where he wrote Jackson a long letter telling all about his trip. He stated in this letter that in Texas the American settlers were twenty to one in favor of annexation of the territory to the United States, and that they were already in virtual rebellion, having driven all Mexican troops from Texas soil. He was confident that nothing but annexation to their mother country would give the Texas colonists ultimate satisfaction. From what source Houston had acquired his apparently definite information is a matter of conjecture. Surely not from Bowie and the Mexicans with whom he had associated at San Antonio; nor from Austin, who at this time had not come to the conclusion that either revolution or annexation would be necessary for Texas; probably from the Whartons, for in 1829 they had written to Houston to ask about the rumor of the revolution that he was supposed to instigate and had expressed a desire to join him in it. Then, too, the Whartons had always been leaders of the "War Party" in Texas, whose object was the separation of Texas from Mexico.

While at Natchitoches Houston also made a report to the War Department of the United States government, concerning his business with the Comanches. The Secretary of War, however, found the report worthless, and refused to pay the expense account of thirty-five hundred dollars that Houston had enclosed. This seems to be reasonable proof that Houston's business, as he said, was a matter of confidence between himself and Jackson, and that the Secretary of War had not been taken into the secret. After he had sent his reports by special messenger from Natchitoches, Houston returned to Nacogdoches.

He had liked this East Texas town so well that he had decided to establish his home there. So he set up his law office and became a citizen of the place in time to be counted in the census of 1833, and to be elected as a representative from that district to a convention of Texas colonists that had been called to meet at San Felipe on April 1. At the convention he lifted his voice to offer a resolution against encroachments on Indian lands, and he took a hand in writing the constitution for the proposed state of Texas upon its separation from Coahuila, a boon that the convention decided to ask in respectful terms of the Mexican government.

On his return to Nacogdoches Houston established himself in the home of the Alcalde of the town, one Adolphus Sterne, an intelligent and broadly-travelled German Jew, whom he had known as a transient inmate of the Nashville Inn. In this home Houston soon won the hearts of all the inmates—the father and mother, the numerous children, even the six-months-old baby. When he became a Roman Catholic, as was obligatory upon all immigrants, Eva Rosine Sterne, the alcalde's young Louisiana wife, stood as godmother, a favor that Houston was never to forget. While in New Orleans for surgical treatment after the battle of San Jacinto, he bought and sent "Madre Mio" a set of handsome jewelry, with the request that it be worn at least one day out of every year "in memory of her godson's affection and of the victory of San Jacinto." The last record we have of these jewels being worn by Mrs. Sterne was when the present state capitol was dedicated on March 2, 1888; she was then a very old lady, but her memory of and her affection for her famous godson remained fresh and true.

At Nacogdoches Houston made many strong and true friendships. One of the most lasting of these attachments was with Colonel Henry Raguet, a Philadelphian of Swiss-French descent, who had immigrated to Nacogdoches with his family. Henry Raguet was an intelligent, well-educated man, a merchant, a large land owner, and a substantial citizen. His was the finest house in town, and he always entertained generously. In this home Houston met the seventeen-year-old daughter, Anna, the pride and joy of her father's heart. This young girl was possessed of a brilliant mind that had been well trained in the best schools of Philadelphia. She was a linguist of ability, being mistress of five languages. When Houston first met her, he had already realized that to be a successful lawyer in Texas a man must know the Spanish language, and he had been seeking a good teacher of the language. Anna undertook the task of tutoring him in this tongue. That he became proficient in Spanish idioms one may well doubt, but the fact stands clear that he learned to adore his young teacher, and for several years he was an ardent suitor for her hand.

With such experiences was Houston's life filled while he lived at Nacogdoches. None of the landmarks of those days remain as memorials except the old stone fort, the stronghold of that frontier settlement.

The Blount home in San Augustine, Texas, where
Sam Houston often visited.
Collection of Col. Andrew Jackson Houston, La Porte, Tex.

THE STEPHEN WILLIAM BLOUNT HOME AT SAN AUGUSTINE

DURING Houston's residence at Nacogdoches he moved about and kept himself informed concerning all that was happening both at home and abroad. He made, during these three years, occasional trips out of Texas, sometimes as far as New York. There, and in other eastern cities, he is known to have transacted business with large land companies in connection with Texas land grants and titles, and, for a while, he was a sort of sub-agent for the Galveston Bay and Texas Land Company. The documents that historians have on hand at present, however, do not give a well-defined account of his relations with this company; that he hoped to build a fine fortune out of negotiations in Texas lands is probable, but the hope was never realized, for soon his time and services were engaged in the prosecution of a former plan of vaster proportions.

Only thirty-five miles from Nacogdoches is the town of San Augustine. From the time of his advent into Texas Houston was as well-known and as much at home in San Augustine as he was in Nacogdoches. There he had many old friends of former days—Elisha Roberts, Philip Sublett, John Cartwright, Dr. Joseph Rowe, George Teal, Stephen William Blount, and a score of others. While on business in San Augustine he usually made his home with Elisha Roberts, for part of the time the alcalde of the town, and the most popular innkeeper in East Texas. The old Roberts Tavern sheltered many of the noted men of Texas—Bowie, Crockett, Travis, Stephen F. Austin, Houston—and it was from the broad gallery, in front, that Mr. Roberts held his alcalde court in 1831. Just "a step down the road" stood the house of Philip Sublett, son-in-law of Roberts. Sublett's house was Houston's second home whenever he chose to stay there, for he and Philip Sublett had been cronies as young men in Tennessee. But these buildings have passed away; probably the only house now standing at San Augustine in which Houston was a familiar guest is the old William Blount house.

This is a beautiful building even today. It still stands, as in the early days, on the corner of Columbia and Ayish streets. It is a one-story house, finely proportioned and beautifully ornamented. The porch, supported by small Corinthian columns, is the most interesting architectural feature of the house as seen from the outside. Colonel Stephen William Blount, its builder, was a delegate to the Convention of March, 1836, a signer of the Declaration of Independence of Texas, and a signer of the constitution. The author of *Texas and Texans* tells us that "while on his way from Washington, Texas, to San Augustine, Colonel Blount met Ratcliff's company on the march to join Houston's army and he joined that company. Only those of this company who had good horses were able to reach San Jacinto in time for the battle, and Stephen W. Blount had the honor of being among these Texas Patriots who stood on the banks of Buffalo Bayou until the arrival of Santa Anna's army, and then marched forth to give them battle . . ."

La Bahia, Goliad. Houston wrote from Goliad, Jan. 17, 1836, to Gov. Henry Smith concerning conditions here. Fannin and his men were massacred March 27, 1836.
Collection of Houston Public Library, Houston, Texas.   J.I. 1935

THE MISSION FORTRESS AT GOLIAD

THE TOWN of Goliad and the old mission fortress at that place figured prominently in the struggle for Texas independence. The ruins of the old fortress are still standing and are a delight to architects as an example of old Spanish buildings, while to Texans, in general, they will always remain a memorial to brave men who died there.

As early as 1722, a fort was erected on the Garcitas river, about five miles above its mouth, on the very site of the stronghold constructed there by La Salle in 1685. Aguayo, the builder of the Spanish fort in 1722, intended it to be a permanent fortification; so he induced Franciscan friars to erect a mission nearby. The mission was called La Bahia del Espiritu Santo. Only four years later, however, both fort and mission were removed to a site near the present town of Victoria, and in 1749, they were transferred to the San Antonio river, where they became the nucleus of the town of Goliad. During all these removals, the mission never changed its name, and the town that grew up about it was called, interchangeably, Goliad for the fort, or La Bahia for the mission.

When Moses Austin came to Texas in 1820, seeking territory on which he might establish a colony, he found only two Mexican settlements within the interior of the province—San Antonio de Bexar and Goliad, both poor, straggling villages. After the Austins had opened the way, other impresarios secured grants for colonization, and by 1828, McMullen and McGloin had staked out a colonial grant that touched La Bahia on one side. The capital of this colony, thirty miles from Goliad, was named San Patricio, while the colony itself was commonly spoken of as the "Irish colony."

After 1830 there was considerable dissatisfaction among the American colonies in Texas, on account of unfair laws and inefficient, tactless administrative officials sent out to them by the Mexican government; in the spring of 1835, however, all was apparently quiet in the province. It is true that Stephen F. Austin, the commissioner who had been sent to Mexico by the

(87)

Convention of 1833 to bear a written statement of their grievances, and to plead for separate statehood for Texas, had been seized while on his way home and had been imprisoned for more than two years in Mexico city, and that resentment had flared hot in the colonies at this ruthless act; but Austin, fearing that their anger at his imprisonment might precipitate his people into a conflict before they were prepared for it, had counselled them to keep quiet and assured them that in due time he would be released. In consequence of this admonition resentment had died out, and in the spring of 1835 all was seemingly quiet in Texas; but it was a quiet like that before the breaking of a storm.

In the summer of that same year the storm clouds lowered. Santa Anna had lashed out and laid waste the Mexican state of Zacatecas, because it had dared to resist his dictatorship; and for fear that Texas might show a similar independence, he had sent his brother-in-law, General Martin Perfecto Cos, with a small army, to keep her quiet. There were good reasons for this step, for it was common knowledge that the radicals, or "War Party," as they were called, were rapidly gaining ground in Texas. Already a young hot-head of that faction, at the head of a band of radicals, had driven out the Mexican garrison from Anahuac. But the Texas people, feeling that William Barrett Travis was hurrying them too swiftly along the road to revolution, denounced his conduct at Anahuac as hasty and unauthorized, and even went so far as to make proclamations of their loyalty to the Mexican government. In a short time, however, the sincerity of this gesture for peace was to be put to the test. The test came when General Cos very foolishly ordered the arrest of Travis and eight other "troublesome Texans." This order swung public opinion definitely on the side of the "War Party." About this time, too, Stephen F. Austin, at last released from prison, arrived in Texas. The momentous question, peace or war, was left for his decision, and he, having studied Santa Anna and the Mexican people at short range for two years, had but one answer, "War! It is our only recourse." Immediately all Texas was united and hasty preparations were made for war.

A provisional government was set up with Henry Smith as governor, and a council composed of a representative from each district in Texas. Austin was put in the field as commander-in-chief of the gathering troops. Houston was sent out by the Department of Nacogdoches as the commander of the East Texas volunteers. Before even this hurried organization could be effected, however, the first clash with the Mexicans had come at Gonzales on October 2, to be quickly followed on the 8th and 10th by skirmishes at Goliad. The battle of Concepción was fought on the 28th. All these small battles had been victories for the Texans, and while they were debating whether or not to lay siege to the stronghold at San Antonio, the new government began to function. Austin, William H. Wharton, and Branch T. Archer were appointed as commissioners to go to the United States to negotiate a loan of a million dollars and to solicit other aid. Houston was appointed the commander-in-chief of the Texas armies in the field, but before the new commander could reach the troops, Ben Milam had led them to San Antonio and had besieged the town. This movement continued from December 5 to 10, when the Texans won another victory and General Cos made a capitulation.

At Goliad on December 20, 1835, ninety-two men met and drew up, adopted, and signed a declaration "that the former province and department of Texas is, and of right ought to be a free, sovereign and independent state." Major Ira Ingram initiated this declaration, but he was aided by Captain Philip Dimmitt's volunteer company, and by the citizens of Goliad. Thirty-one of the signers of this document were citizens of San Patricio and of Refugio. This Goliad Declaration of Independence antedated the general Texas declaration by two months and ten days.

After Texas was cleared of Mexican soldiery in December, 1835, a greater danger threatened: a bitter quarrel developed between the governor and the council, a quarrel that resulted in great harm to Texas. The members of the council were ambitious and greedy for political power; the governor was stubborn, high tempered, and arrogant. Each faction attempted to usurp all the powers of government. The council was able to find military leaders who were so eager for position and glory that they were ready to do its bidding in defiance of the appointments and organization that had been effected by the Consultation which had set up the government itself. Thus Houston's functions and authority as commander were superseded by these ill-advised appointments of the council, and there was no chance for a righting of conditions until the Convention, which had been called for March 1, 1836, should meet.

In the meantime, Santa Anna himself, at the head of an invading army of over five thousand soldiers, appeared at San Antonio on February 23. On March 6, the Alamo fell with the slaughter of all its defenders; but before this event, on March 2, Grant and Morris, with more than a hundred men, were captured at Agua Dulce, a little creek near Patricio. All were brutally shot except Francis W. Johnson and five of his men, who managed to escape. At Goliad, on March 27, Fannin and nearly four hundred men were shot down after a surrender at discretion following the battle of Coleto, fought on March 20. All these disasters to the Texas army were either directly or indirectly the result of the fatal quarrel between the governor and the council, and of the insubordination of military leaders to the orders of the commander-in-chief.

Refugio Mission. Houston came here with the rebellious army under Grant, Jan. 20, 1836. He soon left with his aide, Hockley, for San Felipe.
Collection of the Houston Public Library.

REFUGIO

ABOUT thirty miles south of Goliad is the town of Refugio. There was located the last mission to be constructed by the Franciscan friars in Texas. Its foundations were laid in 1791, but after the secularization of missions in 1794, the friars gave up their work and returned to Spain, leaving the mission of Our Lady of Refuge incomplete. The wild Comanche Indians who roved the country made several depredating raids against the mission settlement, the church services were discontinued, and the mission building fell into decay. As the Irish colonies which were located nearby grew in numbers, the settlers began to push out and build their homes in the country round about the mission ruins, but the majority of the citizens of the village were Mexicans. Such was the condition at Refugio when the Texas revolution broke out in 1835.

In order to show Houston's connection with Refugio, it seems necessary to relate some facts in Texas history that are only indirectly connected with this town or its mission. We have already mentioned the disastrous quarrel between Governor Smith and the Provisional Council, and have stated that the causes of this unfortunate circumstance were jealousy, and ambition on the part of both sides to usurp all the political power in Texas during the four months that they were appointed to rule. The most outstanding subject of this quarrel, however, was what is known as the Matamoras Expedition. Matamoras, a town of some 6,000-8,000 inhabitants, including a considerable number of English and American traders, was situated in the North Mexican state of Tamaulipas, on the Rio Grande, not far from its mouth. This town enjoyed a thriving trade with the interior of Mexico and with the United States. It is said to have had a monthly revenue of more than $100,000.

As early as December 2, 1835, Captain Philip Dimmitt, the commander of the forces at Goliad, had written to the governor and the council, suggesting that the field for the war should be carried from the interior of Texas to the Mexican frontier; he also suggested the taking of Matamoras, for the sake of its rich revenue, which the Texans sorely needed. It was common knowledge that throughout the North Mexican states the Liberal party was strong, and that their hatred for Santa Anna was intense; moreover, the Texans had been informed by several reliable sources that these Mexican Liberals would gladly join them in a war against Santa Anna, provided that Texas would not declare for independence. Many conservatives in Texas believed that this would be the honorable and the wise course for Texas. Therefore, independence had not been declared by the Consultation in November, 1835; that body had simply declared for a return of government under the constitution on 1824.

Although Governor Smith, a strong radical, was opposed to any plan that provided for co-operation with Mexicans—for he had no confidence in any Mexican of whatever type—Houston, with his consent, sent an order to James Bowie on December 17, 1835, ordering him, as its leader, to raise the largest force that he could collect and to set out on the Matamoras expedition. Bowie did not receive the order until near the end of the month, and by that time he had definite information that the time for the success of such a movement—if, indeed, there were ever a time when it might have succeeded—had passed. He gave this information to the government, explaining that his personal scouts on the Rio Grande reported that Santa Anna, seeing the weakness of the Matamoras situation, was hurrying troops to that point. At this same time Bowie expressed his willingness to carry out the commander-in-chief's orders to him, provided they were repeated. By this time, however, another phase of the project had developed at Bexar.

After the Mexicans were withdrawn from San Antonio, there were left in that town, the Alamo being the stronghold, some three or four hundred soldiers, young men who had come from the United States to help Texas fight her battles Among these soldiers was a Scotchman, one Dr. James Grant, who for many years had been a naturalized citizen of Mexico, and whose rich estates near Parras had been confiscated by the Santa Anna government. Dr. Grant was an intelligent, well-educated man, and a Liberal. When the Texas revolution broke out, he joined the Texan army and participated in the taking of Bexar, where he was wounded. After the Mexicans had gone, he began telling the soldiers, who were idling in camps, fine stories about the wealth of Mexico, the willingness of the Mexican Liberals to join the Texans, and the rich booty that might be obtained by an expedition into Mexico; in other words, he preached the Matamoras expedition. By December 31, he had persuaded some two hundred men, including Francis W. Johnson, the commander of the post, to set out with him on this project. Not only did he and Johnson lead the troops from Bexar, but they also took the better part of all the supplies that were at the place—food, clothes, blankets, munitions, medicine.

Johnson, realizing that his authority for doing this thing was doubtful, left Grant to lead the troops as far as Goliad while he went to San Felipe to get the approval of the government for his act. Finding the governor and the council at desperate odds, he decided, at first, to abandon his plans, and so stated to the council, but on the next morning when he returned and announced to that body that he had changed his mind and desired permission to go, they told him that they had already appointed James W. Fannin to take the lead in the Matamoras Expedition, and had made him their "Agent" with authority to appoint whatsoever officers he might need for the project. But the council gave Johnson and Grant permission to continue on the expedition as leaders of the men whom they had brought from Bexar. Thus, the command of the expedition, as authorized by the council, was divided, to say nothing of it as an usurpation of Houston's authority as commander-in-chief of the Texas armies.

Houston, hearing that Johnson and Grant had stripped the post at San Antonio of both men and supplies, went to Goliad to intercept the so-called expedition. There he made the soldiers a speech in which he informed them that the enterprise upon which they were engaged was illegal, because improperly authorized; he also showed them that it would end in a robbing expedition. This speech caused many of the men to refuse to go farther, and some of them were willing to return to San Antonio. Those he sent with Bowie and James Butler Bonham back to the Alamo. Houston himself went on to Refugio, where he ordered the troops arriving at Copano, the nearby seaport, to mobilize under Fannin's command, for while at Goliad he had been informed of the action of the council in superseding his authority by placing Fannin in charge of the Texas army. He made another speech at Refugio and did what he was able to make it clear to the troops that the Matamoras expedition was not a properly authorized movement. But, finding the whole situation hopeless, he returned to San Felipe, wrote a long letter of explanation to the Governor, and asked for a furlough. Smith granted his request and ordered him to go to East Texas to treat with the Indians for a treaty that would keep them neutral while Texas was at war with Mexico. In this enterprise Houston was successful. And we might say that he had been somewhat successful at Refugio, for before he left that town, the citizens had elected him their representative to the Convention which was to meet on March 1.

About a hundred of the soldiers who had set out from Bexar with Johnson and Grant were loyal to those leaders, and would not give up the plan to go to Matamoras. With these men, therefore, the two obstinate leaders pushed on from Goliad to Refugio; there they divided the men into two bands in order to scour the country for horses and provisions with which to continue their project, but before they were ready to march, they were captured and shot by detachments of General Urrea's division of Santa Anna's army of invasion. Grant and some fifty men were killed at the little creek, Agua Dulce; Johnson's band were taken at Refugio. Out of ninety-seven men who were in the two companies, eighty-five were killed. Johnson and five of his men succeeded in making their escape.

The Alamo, San Antonio, Texas, where died on March 6, 1836, its defenders to the last man. "Remember the Alamo" became the battlecry at San Jacinto.

THE ALAMO

HE mission of San Antonio de Valero, commonly called the Alamo, was transplanted from the Rio Grande in 1718 to a site not far from the present location of the old ruins. This mission was an important one, and it contained a mission proper, a presidio, and a village. The church of the mission—the only part now standing—was begun in 1744, but was not finished until 1757. It had twin towers, an arched roof, and a beautiful dome, but these collapsed, through structural weaknesses, in 1762, and, since it was abandoned as a church about that time, the damages were never repaired. The débris from the fallen towers and dome remained in the body of the church until 1848-1850, when the United States government cleared it out and repaired the ruined walls in order that the structure might be used as a quartermaster's department.

The Alamo village had not been greatly prosperous until a consignment of thirteen families from the Canary Islands arrived there in 1731. From this time the colony grew internally, while new colonists arrived from time to time. After the secularization of the missions in 1794, the Alamo lands were divided among the citizens of the village, and from that time on, the inhabitants were ambitiously adding bit by bit to their original lands, and many became rather extensive land owners.

The town that grew up from this mission nucleus was named San Antonio de Bexar, but the natives called it indiscriminately either San Antonio or Bexar. The old mission of San Antonio de Valero, with its enclosing walls and buildings, was occupied in 1805 by the company *del Alamo de Parras*. These soldiers were sent by the Mexican government as a protection to the town against depredating Indians, and by 1810, or 1812, the entire mission property was being called the *Alamo* because of this occupancy.

San Antonio de Bexar was the capital of the province of Texas from 1773 to 1824, when Texas and Coahuila were joined in statehood. San Antonio then lost its importance as a capital, but remained the chief Mexican stronghold in Texas and the head of the local government. Although a number of American colonists went there to live, the town never became a part of any American colony—the Mexicans always continued to dominate there both in population and in political control. Therefore, when the town fell into the hands of the Texans on December 10, 1835, that event not only meant that the Mexicans had lost their foothold in Texas that could be used advantageously as a base for military operations against the colonies, but it was also looked upon as a very humiliating defeat for them to have to surrender a stronghold that had been in their possession for more than a hundred years.

With such a history back of it, it is little wonder that Bexar came to be considered by both the Mexicans and the Texans as "the key to the situation," a place to be held, or to be conquered at all hazards. The Texans had taken it in December, 1835, and they meant to hold it; but they naturally expected that its capture would be the objective of any army of invasion that might come against them. And they were right in their conjectures.

In other sketches we have already told about the disastrous quarrel between the governor and the council, as well as about the fateful Matamoras expedition. It was the Matamoras expedition that had robbed Bexar of three-fourths of its garrison and the best part of the fort's supplies and equipment. After Colonel Francis W. Johnson had left the post, Colonel J. C. Neill became its commander. He had left with him about one hundred men, many of whom were either wounded or sick; moreover, they were desolate, discouraged, indignant; they needed everything—food, medicines for the sick, bedding, blankets and clothes for the coming winter. Neill was in despair; so he began writing to the governor, the council, and the commander-in-chief, telling of the ravage of the post and of its desperate needs. From Goliad, where he had gone to intercept Grant's army, Houston sent to the Alamo thirty men, commanded by James Bowie and accompanied by James Butler Bonham. They reached Bexar on January 19. Governor Smith ordered William Barrett Travis, who had had charge of the recruiting station at San Felipe, to raise a company of one hundred men and go to Neill's assistance. After a great deal of worry and exertion Travis was able to enroll only twenty-five men, but, in obedience to Smith's order, he entered the Alamo with this small group on February 3. On about the 12th or 14th of February David Crockett with from 13 to 17 men also entered the fort. This then, was the force with which this fort had to meet the enemy, 5,000 strong, with Santa Anna himself at their head.

When Houston sent Bowie to the Alamo, he also sent orders —very probably verbal orders, since no written evidence has been found—for Neill to "blow up" the Alamo and remove his forces to Gonzales. The carrying out of these orders was evidently left to the discretion of Bowie, Neill, and other leaders at Bexar. At any rate, Neill soon reported that he did not have a sufficient supply of horses and oxen to carry off his artillery, and the order was not obeyed. About this time, also, Neill was given a furlough in order to visit a sick family, and William Barrett Travis became the commander of the post at San Antonio. The Mexican invading army arrived at Bexar on February 23, with a force outnumbering the Texans twenty-five to one.

The siege began. Fewer than two hundred Texans fought five thousand Mexicans for thirteen days without a single loss, although in a fierce attack on February 25 the Mexicans lost heavily. Again and yet again Travis sent out messengers, pleading for help. He sent many times to Fannin, who was in command of more than five hundred men at Goliad, begging him to come with his whole army, or to send a strong force; but, for one reason or another, no help was sent. On March 1, thirty-two brave men from Gonzales, led by Captain Albert Martin, rode to Bexar and entered the Alamo, although they well knew that the fort was doomed. With the exception of these brave souls, Texas did nothing to carry assistance to the besieged fortress. On March 6, the final attack came, and the Mexicans succeeded in breaking over the walls. They put the Texans to the sword, and not a single white combatant was left alive to tell the story. Mrs. Dickerson, the wife of the captain of artillery, and her fifteen-months-old baby were the only white persons to survive the massacre. Two negro slave boys and about fifteen Mexican women and children were also saved. They were all non-combatants who had sought safety in the fortress upon the arrival of the Mexican army.

The building at Washington, Texas, in which was signed the Declaration of Independence on March 2, 1836.

Collection of Mr. Clarence R. Wharton—Houston

THE HALL OF TEXAS INDEPENDENCE

ACCORDING to the provisions made by the Consultation before its adjournment, an election was held in the Texas Colonies on February 1, 1836, for the selection of delegates to a convention which was to convene at Washington-on-the-Brazos on March 1. The building in which this meeting was held was a new one—still unfinished and unfurnished. It had no window panes, no chairs, no tables; in fact, no comforts or conveniences of any kind. Richard Ellis was elected chairman, and H. S. Kimble was the secretary. A few hours after the convention had been called to order, a wet Texas norther blew up, and the thermometer dropped to 33°. There was no fire in the building and no means of making one; nevertheless, the delegates stubbornly endured all the discomforts, for well they knew that Texas was desperately in need of some kind of stable government, and they had been sent up by the people to plan one. They knew, also, that the Mexican army of invasion was already within the bounds of Texas, and that their little vanguard at Bexar was besieged by many times its number. Almost daily, messengers sent out by Travis were able to slip through the enemy's lines and bear to the governor, to the convention, to the commander-in-chief—to anyone who had authority—the cry for help. Some of the more emotional members of the convention urged that they adjourn and go in a body to the succor of the distressed Alamo. Cooler heads counselled that it would be of greater value to Texas for them to stay at their posts and organize a government than it would for them to sacrifice themselves in a fruitless effort to save the defenders of the Alamo. Therefore, on March 2, 1836, this body passed a resolution declaring Texas a free and independent republic. Sam Houston, sitting as a delegate from Refugio, spoke with logic and power on the wisdom of this resolution. On March 3 the document was signed by the members who were present on that day; Houston's name is on the list. Belated delegates signed the declaration as their credentials were approved.

On March 2, 1836, his forty-third birthday, Houston had been re-elected commander-in-chief of the Texas army. By March 6, he had been able to muster a few men, and on that day, at the very hour when the brave souls at the Alamo were enlisting in the cohorts of Eternity, he set out for Gonzales. It was his plan to gather as large a force as possible and go to the assistance of Travis and his men. First, however, he sent out scouts to ascertain the state of affairs, for he greatly feared that it was already too late to save the Alamo. Travis had promised that so long as he was able to hold the fort, he would fire signal guns both morning and evening; the guns had not been heard for twenty-four hours. Soon rumors began coming that the Alamo had fallen and that all the men had been massacred; and on the evening of the thirteenth, Mrs. Dickerson arrived in Gonzales and confirmed the awful news. That was a black day for Gonzales, for in that one little village, the fall of the Alamo had left thirty women widowed and nearly a hundred children fatherless.

But that was not all the news. Santa Anna had sent a message of defiance, ordering all Texans to surrender and to accept his terms of reconstruction, or suffer the same fate as had been meted out to the men of the Alamo. On the heels of this pronouncement, messengers began coming with the report that the Mexicans were marching on Gonzales. These reports initiated one of the most famous retreats in the annals of America, for it was not merely the retreat of the military forces of Texas: it was the flight of the whole people before an advancing foe. In better days, when their country had been redeemed and they were once more happy in their homes, Texans came to call this experience "The Runaway Scrape."

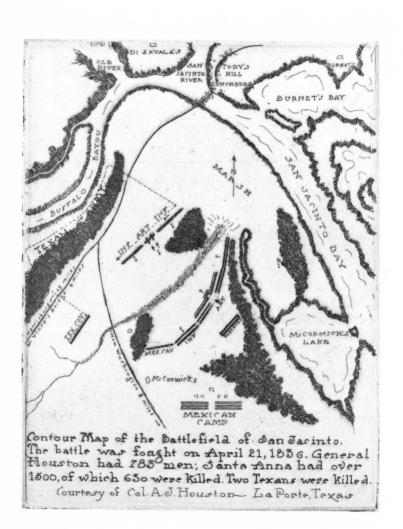

Contour Map of the Battlefield of San Jacinto.
The battle was fought on April 21, 1836. General
Houston had 783 men; Santa Anna had over
1500, of which 630 were killed. Two Texans were killed.
Courtesy of Col. A. J. Houston — La Porte, Texas

The Map of the San Jacinto Battle Field

T HE commander-in-chief, with some three hundred soldiers, left Gonzales in flames on the night of March 13. He was followed by a stream of fleeing women and children, and, in the face of imminent danger of being overtaken by the enemy, he made constant effort to see that all non-combatants were safe before he withdrew his army from any vicinity. This caused a slow retreat, first to the Colorado, then to the Brazos, and midst the rumblings of dissatisfaction—even of mutiny—he pushed slowly on towards Buffalo Bayou, arriving there on April 18. Before the Texan army had left the Brazos, two cannon had come to them as a gift from the citizens of Cincinnati. The soldiers named these cannon the "Twin Sisters."

On April 19, Houston was able to put his soldiers across the river a few miles below Harrisburg, and after an all-night march they went into camp on the morning of the twentieth, just as the sun was rising. Santa Anna with a picked army had marched ahead of Houston along the road to Morgan's Point, or New Washington, and had camped on San Jacinto Creek about three miles above the place. He thought to trap Houston; instead he put himself into the trap, because his only means of escape would have been to cross the river at Lynch's ferry and pass before the Texan camp. Houston even stood by and allowed the enemy to receive reinforcements—he said, at a later time, "so as not to have to take more than one bite at the cherry."

There is a great deal that might be told in connection with the battle that was soon fought, but since these details are an oft-told tale in Texas, we shall omit them here. For our purpose it is enough to say that on April 21, 1836, the battle of San Jacinto was fought and won by the Texans. Strangely enough, the Texas signal for the attack had been a popular love song—"Will You Come to My Bower"—played on a fife. But it was quickly followed by a battle cry that froze the very heart blood of the Mexicans with terror, "Remember the Alamo! Remember Goliad!" Well did those Mexican soldiers know that a people who remembered the Alamo and Goliad would scarcely remember to be merciful to the foe who had perpetrated those brutal massacres. The Mexicans lost on that day six hundred and thirty, killed; two hundred and eight, wounded; and over five hundred prisoners. They also lost a large quantity of arms, a great number of mules and horses, their camp equipment, and a military chest containing twelve thousand dollars. The Texan loss was eight killed and twenty-five wounded.

While leading the battle in its onward rush, Houston was severely wounded in the ankle, and the wound was so painful that he was obliged to retire. Santa Anna was captured on the following day. As battles go, San Jacinto was not a great one; neither side had large numbers in the engagement; it was not long fought. But the result was momentous: it assured the independence of Texas, and it rid her of all Mexican soldiery, for Santa Anna was forced to order Filisola, his second in command, to withdraw all Mexican troops from Texas soil.

Santa Anna was captured on April 22nd, and
brought before the wounded Houston.
Collection of Hon. Lawrence Y. Sherman, Daytona Beach, Fla.

Wd
after
Haddle
1935

Huddle's Picture of Santa Anna's Surrender

N THE west wall of the capitol of Texas, at the south entrance, hangs a painting by William H. Huddle. It represents Santa Anna as he was brought before Houston on April 22, 1836. Houston's wounded ankle had pained him all night, and he had not been able to rest; next day, however, stretched out on a blanket under a large moss-hung oak, he had been able to forget the painful wound and the horrors of the battle in blessed sleep. Suddenly he was awakened by a blur of sounds; then articulate words came from a group of Mexican prisoners huddled over a camp fire,—"El Presidente, El Presidente!" Early that morning detachments had been sent out to scour the country for the purpose of taking straggling prisoners. A party of five had turned away from Vince's Bayou to search more carefully down the Buffalo Bayou, and one of the party, James A. Sylvester, saw a lone Mexican making his way to a small bridge. Sylvester called to his companions, and soon they overtook the straggler, who had fallen flat in the grass and had covered his head with an old blanket. The man was poorly dressed and carried no arms; he said that he was a private soldier, but the Texans spied handsome jewelled studs on his shirt front and knew that he was no private.

After his identity had been revealed by his own soldiers, Santa Anna asked to be carried to Houston. Approaching the commander-in-chief, he addressed him, saying: "I am General Antonio Lopez de Santa Anna, and a prisoner of war at your disposition." Houston looked at him keenly, and by a motion of his hand directed him to a tool-chest, where he might sit down. Santa Anna took the proffered seat and immediately proposed to enter into negotiations for his liberation; but Houston answered that it was a subject concerning which he had no authority, inasmuch as Texas had a government to which such matters belonged. The captured general in a vain and pompous manner replied: "Ah, General Houston, you can afford to be generous; you are born to no common destiny— you have conquered the Napoleon of the West." But both Houston and Thomas J. Rusk, the Texan Secretary of War, assured him that no negotiations could be opened until the Texas cabinet had assembled.

Before Santa Anna retired from the interview. however, Houston told him that he must order his second in command, General Vicente Filisola, to evacuate Texas and fall back to Monterey. There was nothing for Santa Anna to do but to obey, and Deaf Smith carried the message to Filisola. This, briefly, is the story of Santa Anna's surrender.

Huddle's painting endeavors to portray the moment that Santa Anna introduced himself to Houston. The artist may not stand high among the painters of the world, but in his "Surrender of Santa Anna" he tried faithfully to present conditions as they existed. For his figures he used actual photographs or portraits of the participants in the scene, and in order to make his setting true to history, he interviewed many eye-witnesses of the event. So whether his picture meets praise or adverse criticism from art critics, Huddle has done something no other artist has attempted; at least, we must all concede that the spirit of his picture is inspirational. In 1901 the state of Texas bought the painting from the artist for the sum of $4,000.

The Steamer "Yellowstone," on which sailed President Houston and his Cabinet with the body of Stephen F. Austin. The burial was at Peach Point, Brazoria County. Collection of Mrs. Leita Small, Custodian of the Alamo......

CAPT. W. GRAYSON

THE STEAMBOAT YELLOWSTONE

NOTHER interesting incident connected with the battle of San Jacinto concerns the steamboat *Yellowstone*. This was a cotton boat owned and usually commanded by Captain Thomas W. Grayson. On April 12, 1836, however, when Houston commandeered the craft to enable him to put his army across the Brazos, Captain John Ross, the first mate, was in command. At this time the *Yellowstone* was on its way up the Brazos to Groce's Landing for a load of cotton. Houston ordered the boat to be brought to him empty, but as Captain Ross insisted that cotton bales would serve both as ramparts in case of fire from the enemy, and as needed ballast, Houston consented to the cargo. By the 13th Ross and his crew had successfully landed the army and all the equipage across the river. Houston pledged the captain and his men that for this service they should be eligible for donation and bounty lands on the same terms as enlisted soldiers and their officers, but in the fifties, long after the death of Ross, his widow was still memorializing the Texas Legislature for payment of the pledge, and Houston was certifying in her behalf that without the timely service rendered by Ross and the *Yellowstone*, the victory at San Jacinto would never have been won.

But this was not the only service rendered by this boat and its gallant captain. On April 28, 1836, it bore the *ad interim* president, David G. Burnet, and his cabinet to the San Jacinto battlefield, where peace parleys were held with Santa Anna. It was this boat, also, that carried the governmental officials, Houston, and Santa Anna to Galveston, and after leaving Houston there to take a sloop to New Orleans, the *Yellowstone* carried the other officials to Velasco.

Indeed, the *Yellowstone* did noble duty for the new republic; but the service for which patriotic Texans love best to remember her is the trip she made down the Brazos from Columbia to Peach Point, bearing to the grave the body of Stephen F. Austin, the Father of Texas.

"Orozimba", residence of Dr. James A. E.
Phelps, near Columbia, Texas. Houston
visited Santa Anna here in Oct., 1836.
Collection of Mrs. E. E. Norfleet, Houston

Orozimba, the Phelps Home

N April 28, 1836, President Burnet and his cabinet, aboard the *Yellowstone*, arrived at the San Jacinto battlefield from Galveston, where they had taken refuge a few days before. These governmental officials took charge of matters pertaining to the final peace terms with Santa Anna. General Houston was granted a leave of absence in order that he might go to New Orleans to have his wound treated. Thomas J. Rusk was appointed the commander-in-chief of the army. On May 8 the government established itself at Velasco, where treaties were executed with Santa Anna, who, though a prisoner, still represented Mexico. The Mexican army of 7,000 troops continued its retreat from Texas soil, finally crossing the Rio Grande in the early days of June.

The Texas army stubbornly determined to execute Santa Anna, but Houston, as well as other more conservative men, believed that Santa Anna would be of greater value to Texas alive than dead. But feeling ran so high over the matter that *El Presidente* was actually seized by the army, and only the earnest pleas of the government officials saved him from the same fate that he had meted out to hundreds of Texans. In order to be safe, the man had to be closely guarded. For this purpose he became a guest at Orozimba, the plantation home of Dr. James A. E. Phelps, which was situated near the town of Columbia on the Brazos. So great was his fear and melancholy while at this hospitable home that Santa Anna had to be saved from death at his own hands three times by the jovial doctor and his sympathetic wife. Santa Anna was truly grateful for this kindness, for in 1842, when Orlando, the young son of this household, was in a Mexican prison on account of his participation in the Mier expedition, Santa Anna pardoned him, set him free, gave him money, and saw to it that the young man reached home in safety. Santa Anna also expressed gratitude to Houston, to whom he claimed that he owed his life. At Santa Anna's invitation Houston visited him at Orozimba, and while there he arranged for his former enemy to be sent to Washington, D. C., upon his release by the Texas government. While at

Washington Santa Anna met Andrew Jackson and many other prominent Americans. Many who had looked upon Santa Anna, the President of Mexico, as an inhuman monster, on account of the horrible massacres that he had ordered upon captured Texans, came to like the man because of his charming manners.

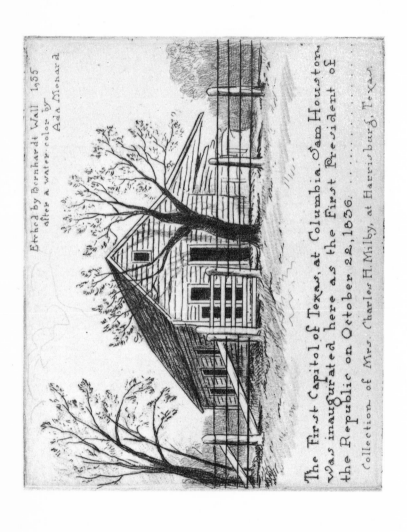

Etched by Bernhardt Wall 1935
after a water color by
Ada Menard

The First Capitol of Texas, at Columbia. Sam Houston
was inaugurated here as the First President of
the Republic on October 22, 1836. . . . .

Collection of Mrs. Charles H. Milby, at Harrisburg, Texas

THE TEXAN CAPITOL AT COLUMBIA

HE Texans realized that the sooner they organized a permanent government, the greater would be their safety and the more quickly would they react from the demoralization of war. So, in September, 1836, the constitution that had been drawn up by the convention in March was submitted to the people for ratification. At the same time the constitution was sent to the people, the question of whether or not Congress should have the power to amend the constitution was also submitted to their vote. At this time, too, the people were called upon to elect a president, a vice president, fourteen senators, and twenty-nine representatives. The election returns showed that the constitution had been ratified but the right to amend it had been withheld from Congress. Houston was elected president and Mirabeau B. Lamar was the vice president.

The first Congress of the Republic met at Columbia on the Brazos on the twenty-second day of October, 1836. Sam Houston was inaugurated and took his seat as president. He immediately appointed his two opponents in the race for the presidency—Stephen F. Austin and Henry Smith—to the two most important cabinet offices, Austin as Secretary of State, and Smith as Secretary of the Treasury. At this time the public debt was a million and a quarter dollars. The treaties that had been made by Santa Anna were repudiated by the Mexican government, and the danger of another invasion was a constant threat. Houston's task was colossal; he had to organize the new government so as to be ever on guard against the enemy, and at the same time to promote economic security and internal prosperity.

The housing facilities at Columbia were entirely inadequate for the various departments of the new government. None of the comforts and few of the necessities for the promotion of efficient work were provided; nevertheless, this little town saw very busy days and very earnest workers at the so-called capitol.

1935

Etched by Bernhardt Wall, in Texas,
from a Painting by
Jennie Hunter.

STEPHEN F. AUSTIN.

"The Father of Texas is no more. The First
Pioneer of the Wilderness has departed.
General Stephen F. Austin, Secretary of
State, expired this Day." President Sam
Houston's announcement, on Dec. 27, 1836.

Stephen Fuller Austin, the Father of Texas

N STEPHEN FULLER AUSTIN, Houston found the greatest Texas patriot and a truly great man. Utterly unselfish wherever the interests of Texas were concerned, Austin immediately buried his own disappointment and humiliation at his failure to become the first elected president of the republic, for the foundation of which he had given the best years of his life, and accepted with pride the position of Secretary of State, because that office gave him the chance still to direct the course and to help shape the destiny of his beloved Texas. When fifteen years before this time he had given his promise to a dying father to carry on and to bring to fruition his dreams and plans of planting a colony in the territory called Texas, he had given up whatever ambitions and plans he may have had for his own life. He kept his word to the letter; he did his utmost to become a good impresario for the projected colonies. He brought out his first colonists in 1821, and by 1836 he had settled more than 1500 families. He had watched Texas rapidly increase until it could boast of a population of perhaps 35,000 souls, not counting the 20,000 roving Indians. Now that these colonial groups had won for themselves independence and had set up a nation of their own, there was more work than ever to be done. The whole machinery of government had to be installed and co-ordinated. It was a real patriot's job, and Austin buried himself in it.

The quarters in the capitol at Columbia were lacking in all the comforts and the facilities for office routine. Notwithstanding the poor conditions of his surroundings, Austin, always a man of delicate health, labored long hours in fireless rooms, giving little thought to the requirements of his frail body. He contracted a cold which quickly developed into an attack of pneumonia that caused his death on December 27, 1836.

Grave of Stephen F. Austin, Gulf Prairie Cemetery at Peach Point, Brazoria County, Texas. The body was taken to Austin Oct. 1910.
Collection of Mrs. Hally Bryan Perry

Austin's Tomb

P RESIDENT Houston's proclamation of Stephen F. Austin's passing was terse and generous. It was written on the day of Austin's death as follows: "The Father of Texas is no more. The First Pioneer of the wilderness has departed. General Stephen F. Austin, Secretary of State, expired this day." As Father of Texas, Austin will ever be remembered. "For fifteen years," says Dr. Eugene C. Barker, "he held the destiny of Texas in the hollow of his hand, and characteristically his last conscious thought was for its welfare."

Austin died at the age of forty-three. President Houston, his cabinet, and a host of friends escorted the body, aboard the steamboat *Yellowstone*, to Peach Point, the home of Austin's sister, and interred it with full military honors in the family burial ground. Austin once wrote: "I think I derive more satisfaction from a view of flourishing farms springing up in the wilderness, than military or political chieftains do from the retrospect of their victorious campaigns. My object is to build up for the present as well as for future generations." This great man did build nobly and well for his own generation, but he built as truly for future generations, and Texans yet to be born will bow in pride and reverence at the sound of his name.

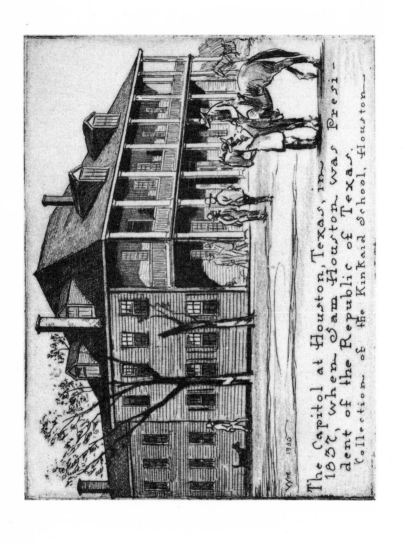

The Capitol at Houston, Texas, in 1857, when Sam Houston was President of the Republic of Texas.
Collection of the Kinkaid School, Houston

The Texas Capitol at Houston

THE SEAL of Texas was adopted by the First Congress while it was sitting at Columbia. There, also, the flag bearing a single five-pointed star was chosen. But after three months of arduous labor this First Congress of the Republic of Texas adjourned to hold its next session in Houston, to which city the capital was moved for the sake of better accommodations. Houston was a new town just being laid out in town lots, and the accommodations for the government, though better than they had been at Columbia, were nevertheless very crude. But the people were inspired by the realization of their independence as a nation; they would develop; they would grow; and they would become great and acquire wealth and comforts and even luxuries. It mattered little to them that their homes, or even their capitol, should be considered crude or inadequate. In his first message President Houston had said: "We now occupy the proud attitude of a sovereign and independent Republic, which will impose upon us the obligation of evincing to the world that we are able to be free." That seemed to be the keynote of the Texans' desire—to evince to the world that they, as a people, were able, were worthy to be free.

The United States recognized the independence of Texas on March 3, 1837. This recognition was one of the last acts signed by Andrew Jackson as President. One can well imagine that it gave him more pleasure than anything he had done for the past ten years, for was it not the fulfillment of the plans of his old favorite? And was not Houston president of the new Republic? Only one step in the plan was still to be taken, but that would surely come in due time. No doubt the old man hoped to live to see, to help effect, that next step—the annexation of Texas to the United States.

The town of Houston remained the capital of Texas until 1840, when the seat of government was permanently transferred, except in periods of danger from Mexican or Indian raids, to Austin on the Colorado. In times of danger, however, Houston or Washington-on-the-Brazos again became the temporary capital.

(129)

On the site of the old capitol building in Houston there stands today the block-long, magnificent structure known as the Rice Hotel. Probably in all their pride in being free and sovereign people, the men who sat and worked in that old capitol from 1837 to 1840 were never able to visualize their crude shacks grown into skyscrapers, or their muddy, boggy streets—mere paths—broadened into great teeming thoroughfares. But they carried on; they did their part in "evincing to the world that they were able and worthy to be free."

"The White House", the Presidential Residence of Sam Houston, at Houston, Texas, while the seat of Government was at that place, 1837

Collection of Mrs. Robt. A. John.

THE TEXAS WHITE HOUSE

ONLY a few blocks to the southeast of the capitol, President Houston's residence stood. This house was jocularly called the "White House." Some wag had said: "Andrew Jackson, the President of the United States, lives in a mansion called the White House, so why should Sam Houston's mansion not be named in honor of that of his old chieftain?" John Audubon, the great naturalist, was one of many who visited Texas out of curiosity or the necessity of transacting business during Houston's first administration. He gives us this description of the Texas White House: "We approached the President's mansion, wading in mud and water above our ankles. This abode is a small log house, consisting of two rooms and a passage through, after the Southern fashion . . . . The President being engaged in the opposite room, a stroll about the city was suggested . . . . Returning we were presented to his Excellency who wore a velvet suit and a cravat something in the style of Seventy-six. The President asked his visitors to drink with him, which we did, wishing success to the Republic."

In one of the rooms of this log house there were two beds. One was for President Houston; the other was for Ashbel Smith, the surgeon general of the Republic of Texas.

Home of Ashbel Smith, M.D., at Evergreen now Goose Creek Texas, visited by Sam Houston. Dr. Smith was the Texan Minister to the Court of St. James and the Court of St. Cloud. From the "Biographical Sketch of of Ashbel Smith, M.D.," by Dr. S.C. Red, 1929. Courtesy of The Houston Public Library

"Evergreen," Ashbel Smith's Plantation Home

ASHBEL SMITH was probably one of the best friends that Houston had during his career in Texas; certainly he was one of his most useful co-workers during his first administration as president. In fact, this man, Ashbel Smith, played many parts in Texas history. He was a planter, a statesman, a diplomat, and one of the most famous physicians of the times. Born of illustrious American parentage at Hartford, Connecticut, on August 13, 1805, he was given the best educational advantages that could be had in America and the youth made good use of his opportunities, for before his twentieth birthday he had received from Yale College both the B. A. and the M. A. degrees. He began the study of law, but ill health forced him to seek a milder climate. He went to North Carolina, where he continued to study law; but his health failed entirely and he was forced to give up his work. While he was convalescing, he became interested in the science of medicine and decided to devote his life to that study. In this branch of learning he received his training in the best schools of both the United States and Europe.

In 1836 he became interested in the Texas revolution, and in the early months of 1837 he emigrated to the new republic. He became an intimate friend of Sam Houston, who appointed him surgeon general of the Texas army. From that time to the day of his death, he rendered Texas a varied service: from 1842 to 1845 he was the Texan minister to England and France; in 1846 he served as a surgeon in General Taylor's army in Mexico; in 1856 he represented Harris county in the Texas legislature; in 1861 he entered the Confederate army with the rank of captain, but was soon made colonel of the Second Texas Infantry; in 1866 he was again in the Texas legislature; and in 1878 he was the commissioner sent from Texas to the Paris Exposition.

During all these years Dr. Smith never gave up his study or his practice of medicine. He attended many of the great medical conventions of the United States and was a constant contributor to the best medical journals. The members of his profession regarded him as the outstanding authority on the treatment of yellow fever. But of all his services to Texas he himself regarded the part that he had in the establishment of the University of Texas as the crowning accomplishment.

Ashbel Smith was never married, but he bought two thousand acres of land on Galveston Bay and established a plantation which he called "Evergreen." There he erected a comfortable but unpretentious house in which he entertained his many friends and neighbors. During his life at Evergreen he did a great deal of charity practice among the needy. But he is said to have exercised true "Yankee" thrift in the management of his affairs, although he lived well while he was laying up a considerable fortune. His plantation today has become the center of the famous Goose Creek oil field.

Such was the man whom Houston selected to be his house-mate, his physician, his confidential friend.

Capitol, Austin, from 1839 to 1856, and connected with the activities of Gen. Houston while President. Collection of the Kinkaid School, Houston.

THE FIRST CAPITOL AT AUSTIN

ON JANUARY 14, 1839, President Lamar signed an act which created a commission to select a site for a permanent capital city for the Republic of Texas. The commission chose the site of the small village of Waterloo, situated on the north bank of the Colorado river. This location is about the center of the state of Texas as its boundaries lie today, but in 1839 it was on the frontier of the settled portions of the Republic. The stockade that surrounded the first capitol building in Austin was not merely an object of adornment; it was an all-too-necessary precaution against Indian raids that were frequent in the frontier capital.

In September of 1841, Houston was again elected President of Texas with Edward Burleson as Vice President. In 1842 a Mexican army invaded Texas and captured San Antonio, Goliad, and Refugio. The members of the district court which was in session at San Antonio at the time were carried away as prisoners to Mexico. Although the invaders remained only a few days, the event aroused all Texas. Houston called a special session of Congress to meet at Houston, as Austin, on the frontier, was considered an unsafe meeting place for the deliberating body. This Congress passed an act declaring war on Mexico, but Houston promptly vetoed it, because of an absolutely depleted treasury, entire unpreparedness of the military, and no hope of raising funds sufficient to create an adequate army, equip it, put it in the field, and pay the soldiers for their services. Notwithstanding these very evident reasons for avoiding a state of war, the president's veto gave his enemies an excuse for a great deal of criticism of, and unjustifiable propaganda against, his administration. Andrew Jackson, however, wrote to his friend, congratulating him on the veto and calling it an act of bravery and wisdom.

The French Embassy at Austin, Texas, residence of Monsieur de Saligny, President Sam Houston matched wits with the English and French until 1844.

Collection of Mrs Lucy Belle Norfleet, Houston.

THE FRENCH EMBASSY AT AUSTIN

DURING Houston's second administration as President of the Republic of Texas, he had to give much of his time and attention to foreign relations. The United States recognized the independence of Texas in 1837. In 1839, France followed this example, and when Mexico protested, the President of the French Council replied that his government had made a "mature and impartial study of the situation," and had satisfied itself "that the existence of Texan independence was an accomplished fact, against which all efforts of Mexico would be unable to prevail"; therefore, France would be compelled to look out for her own interests and sign treaties of amity and trade with the new nation. From this time on France was very friendly to Texas, and her support and her example were of great value. Holland and Belgium followed the action of France and recognized the new republic in 1840.

But England, the most important of all the European nations so far as Texan interests were concerned, delayed recognition. Concerning Texas, England's interests were somewhat complicated, and we shall not attempt to go into detail concerning them; but it is safe to say that two of the reasons why she delayed to admit Texas into the fraternity of nations were: she wished to make a bargain that Texas would abolish the slave trade in return for her recognition; and she feared that her recognition of the new nat on would precipitate its annexation to the United States, an event she desired to forestall if possible But after France, Holland, and Belgium had negotiated for treaties of trade and amity with Texas, England was practically forced, for the sake of her trade interests, to recognize the young republic. Consequently in November, 1840, she entered into two treaties with the Texas government, one for trade and amity, the other for the suppression of the slave trade in Texas. The first of these reached Texas in due time and was duly signed and ratified; but for some reason the second was delayed in transit and was not ratified immediately, whereupon the English government withheld ratification of the first treaty until the second was also ready. For this reason, formal recognition of the Republic of Texas was not made by England until June, 1842.

Finally recognized by the leading governments of the world as a free and independent nation, Texas still found herself with many problems to solve concerning international contacts. Some of these problems had to do with the making of further treaties that would advance the trade and diplomatic interests of the republic, others were concerned with finance, and between the United States and Texas there was the burning question of annexation. Immediately following the victory at San Jacinto, the Texas government *ad interim* under David G. Burnet had dispatched commissioners to the United States with instructions to broach the subject of annexation as well as that of recognition. These gentlemen, faithful to their instructions, wrote a letter in the following July to the American Secretary of State proposing to incorporate their newly organized republic with that of the United States. Two months later the people of Texas, by an almost unanimous vote, pronounced in favor of annexation. But the United States dallied with the proposition, and whenever it was pushed to a vote in the Congress, it failed to pass. The sectional question of slavery was already rearing its ugly head in the legislative bodies of the United States. A strong anti-slavery group was opposed to the annexation of Texas, since its geographical location would tend to make of this new territory, if it were incorporated into the United States, a stronghold for the spread of slavery. Chagrined at the attitude of the United States in regard to annexation, Houston felt compelled to "coquette" in politics with the European nations; and in the matter of annexation, or no annexation, he played no mean hand in the international game.

As has been intimated, it was clearly to the interest of the European nations for Texas to remain independent of the United States, on account of the tariff question. But Mexico had continued to refuse to recognize Texan independence, and Texas was too weak to protect herself from the devastating raids that Mexico had made and constantly threatened. Texas had to have a protector; she had sought that protector in the United States through annexation, but had been rejected or put off to a more convenient season for a discussion of the matter. At this time Houston began negotiations with the

European powers for this needed protection. This "coquetting" with the European nations, as Houston called his diplomatic energy, may have had much to do with hurrying the United States to a decision to accept the offer of Texas to become a state of the Union. During some five or six years, however, diplomatic relations were a lively subject, and the nations of Europe as well as the United States were careful to keep their diplomatic agents in the new republic. France, however, was the only nation that bought and owned its own embassy.

In 1842-1843, Count Alphonse de Saligny, the French Chargé d'Affaires to Texas, built on a beautiful hill in east Austin a story and a half frame house, which at that time was one of the finest buildings in the capital. This old "French Embassy," now the private residence of an Austin woman, still stands on Robinson Hill, an historic relic of the days when Texas was listed as one of the independent nations of the world.

MRS. SAM HOUSTON
(MARGARET MOFFETTE LEA)
Collection of Col. A. J. Houston, La Porte, Tex.

A Picture of Mrs. Houston—Margaret Lea

LTHOUGH Houston had been disappointed in his first marriage, he had not lost faith in the value of the institution as a means for promoting human happiness. For several years after his arrival in Texas he had loved and courted Anna Raguet, the brilliant young daughter of Colonel Henry Raguet of Nacogdoches. A number of fine letters that he wrote to her during this period are still in existence, to reveal to us many of the man's social characteristics. While wounded on the battlefield of San Jacinto, he fashioned a wreath of laurel leaves to send to the adored Anna with these words: "These are laurels that I send you from the field of San Jacinto. Thine, Houston." But the girl was ultimately lost to him because of the babblings of idle tongues that presented some of the general's past experiences in a bad light, and it was his own intimate friend and Secretary of State, Dr. Robert A. Irion, who finally married Anna Raguet. But the laurels from San Jacinto are still cherished by the charming Anna's descendants, and she named her first-born son Sam Houston Irion.

In 1839 Houston made a business trip to Alabama. Naturally, the hero of San Jacinto was the object of lavish hospitality, and in Mobile he chanced to meet William Bledsoe, who invited him for a week-end visit in his country home. Mrs. Bledsoe had as her guest on this occasion her sister, Margaret Lea. Houston fell in love with the girl, and when he left the Bledsoe home, Margaret Lea had promised to marry him.

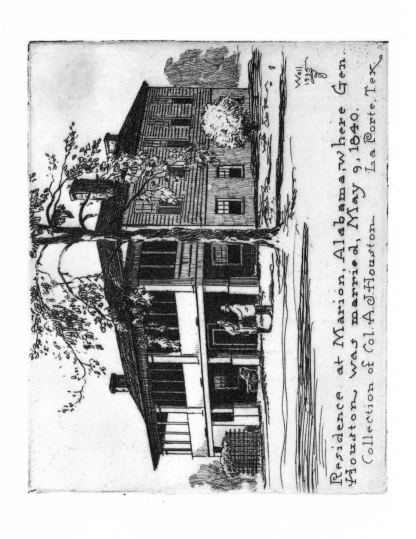

Residence at Marion, Alabama, where Gen.
Houston was married, May 9, 1840.
Collection of Col. A.J.Houston   La Porte, Tex.

The Lea Home at Marion, Alabama

UPON Houston's return to Texas after his visit to Alabama, he was violently enraged because of President Lamar's war upon the Cherokee Indians in East Texas. He made a speech at Nacogdoches concerning this war that alienated many of his staunchest friends—men like Thomas J. Rusk, Henry Raguet, and Adolphus Sterne—for they had approved of and participated in the Indian war. Notwithstanding their indignation at Houston's harsh words, these very men whom he had berated as cowards and as murderers of his old friend, Chief Bowles, elected him to a seat in the Texas Congress from their district. Houston's hold upon the hearts of Texans was secure; they could never long forget his heroism and his victory at San Jacinto. Besides these more or less elusive merits, they recognized his ability as a statesman, and well they knew that all his talents were sorely needed by the growing nation. Such was, and continued to be, the attitude of the majority of Texans toward Sam Houston.

So in 1839-1840 he was a very busy man, too busy for the fine art of making love. He had come, however, to the point in his life, in his career, when he wanted a home; he wanted a wife and children; he was ready to settle down at the head of a family. Consequently, he implored Margaret Lea to come to Texas for their marriage. Because of her great love for and understanding of this man, Margaret was willing to accede to his wishes, but her mother said, "No," and said it very emphatically. Mrs. Lea was by no means pleased with the selection of a husband that her daughter Margaret had made; so she herself, accompanied by kinsmen, decided to go to Texas to "spy out the land" for the sake of financial investments, and also to investigate thoroughly the situation and the conditions into which the confiding Margaret was so willing to walk blindly. Houston, thinking that his fiancée was accompanying her mother, met the boat at the wharf at Galveston, but in answer to his eager question, "Where is Margaret?" Mrs. Lea replied: "She is at her home where she ought to be; and I can tell you frankly, Sam Houston, that when my daughter is married, the ceremony will be performed in my own home in Marion, Alabama." In the face of such a pronouncement, there was but one thing to do. Busy or not, Sam Houston had to go to Alabama to get his wife.

There were others who had serious objections to this marriage, and they did what they could to prevent it. Houston's old and tried friends, Ashbel Smith and Barnard E. Bee, implored him to forego marriage forever. They argued that his temperament, his habits, ill-fitted him for happiness in wedlock; they even boldly predicted that he would not live with any wife for a longer period then six months. But Houston was determined to have a home; so he went for his bride, and on May 9, 1840, at the Lea home in Marion, Alabama, Sam Houston and Margaret Moffatt Lea were married. A happy married life of twenty-three years was to prove that good and wise men can be poor prophets.

The Independence Home of Gen. Sam Houston—
Mrs. Houston lived here after the General's death—

Collection of Col. A. J. Houston.

La Porte, Tex.

Houston's Home at Independence

N DECEMBER, 1841, Houston found himself again President of the Republic of Texas. When he left that high office in December, 1838, he was by no means a popular man in the political circles of Texas, for he had not been able—nor had he tried—to please the various ambitious and clamoring factions. During Lamar's administration, however, Texas had not prospered. The public debt had increased abnormally, and various visionary schemes of the poetic-minded president had failed; therefore, not only his old and true friends, but even many of his enemies and critics, as well, were eager to put Houston back in the chief executive's office.

His first official act as president was the initiation of a policy of the strictest economy, reducing all salaries and abolishing all unnecessary offices. Small as it already was, he cut his own salary in half. Payment of many claims was postponed so that the depleted treasury could have a chance to survive. But in spite of the harshest measures for saving, in spite of the deepest cuts in the national expenditure, the public debt went on increasing. Largely because of Houston's sagacity and personal magnetism, however, throughout all these hard times the nation gave every evidence of a continual and rapid growth. A leader with such heavy burdens upon him as Houston was forced to carry during these times, needs in his leisure moments relaxation and surcease from cares of state. The president found this solace in the bosom of his growing family.

His private home was at Independence. There, too, his mother-in-law, who had come to think that her daughter Margaret had not been so short-sighted in the choice of a husband, had set up her home upon her removal from Alabama to Texas. There good schools had been established and were developing into active and sound educational institutions. In fact, this little town of Independence arrogated to itself the title of the "Athens of Texas." It was a pleasant place to live, and there Houston was satisfied and happy.

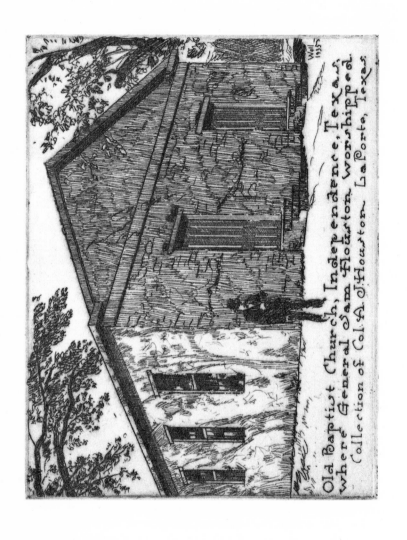

Old Baptist Church, Independence, Texas, where General Sam Houston worshipped. Collection of Col. A. J. Houston, LaPorte, Texas

THE OLD BAPTIST CHURCH AT INDEPENDENCE

HE HOUSTONS of America had been Presbyterians for many generations. When Elizabeth Houston left her Virginia home to trek across the mountains to a Tennessee wilderness, she said that the greatest hardship in making this change was in leaving her home church and the Presbyterian community in which she had lived from childhood. And in the new home we find her one of the charter members of the Maryville Presbyterian church, a house of worship that has been noteworthy in the annals of Presbyterianism for a hundred years and an organization that remains famous to this day. In this wilderness church the mother of Houston worked and worshipped; with the help of its counsel she "reared her children in the fear and admonition of the Lord." She instilled in their minds the doctrines of the Calvinistic faith and put them through the task of memorizing the catechism of her belief. There is little wonder, then, that throughout his life, Sam Houston constantly quoted or referred to the Bible as the highest authority; that attitude had been ingrained into his subconscious mind during his youth. But as a young man he had never become a communicant of the church.

Once during the bitterest experience of his life, just after his separation from Eliza Allen, in repentance and despair at the wreck of his happiness, he sought consolation at the throne of Grace, and asked for baptism at the hands of a Presbyterian minister. His request was taken under advisement, but worldly considerations—the feelings of Eliza's family—brought an adverse decision concerning the matter, and for a time he was as true a pagan as the Indians among whom he lived.

After his arrival in Texas he joined the Roman Catholic Church out of political policy and necessity—"Muldoon Catholics," such persons were called. After his marriage to Margaret Lea, he came within the Christian influence of his wife and her mother. Mrs. Lea and her daughter were most ardent Baptists, lay workers in the field. They believed that perfect happiness for the Houston family could never be attained until the husband

and father joined the Baptist church. This end was not accomplished, however, until November 19, 1854, when the Reverend Rufus C. Burleson baptized Senator Sam Houston in Rocky Creek near the town of Independence. From this time forth he was a regular if not a consistent member of the Baptist church at Independence. Houston himself often remarked, in later days, that he and his pocketbook were both baptized on that day, for it was common knowledge that he was regularly called upon to pay more than half of his pastor's salary. When he was in Washington, the senator attended the Baptist church on E Street. During the sermon he usually whittled on a soft pine board, fashioning some trinket, a pair of entwined hearts, an anchor and chain, or perhaps a cross and crown, which he would present to some child at the close of the service; but in the afternoon he wrote Mrs. Houston a résumé of the morning sermon.

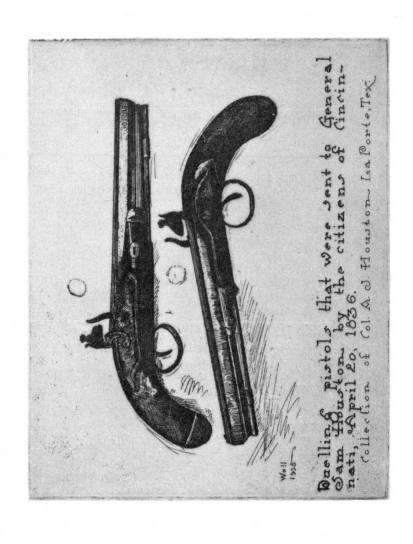

Duelling pistols that were sent to General
Sam Houston by the citizens of Cincin-
nati, April 20, 1836.
Collection of Col A J Houston LaPorte,Tex

HOUSTON'S DUELLING PISTOLS

HOUSTON'S entire life might be described by one word—*stormy*. He always had many true friends, but he had many enemies, as well, and at times he took no pains to conciliate them. On the other hand, he did and said many things calculated to stir up jealousy, resentment, and animosity towards himself and his followers. Probably one of the potent causes of much of the criticism and animosity that at different times flared hotly against the man, was a quality of secretiveness in his nature; he usually kept his own counsel when important matters were afoot, until the very moment for the performance of an act. No doubt, this characteristic had been acquired or strengthened by his sojourn among the Indians; at any rate, it often antagonized co-workers who considered it too strong an indication of the power of a dictator. A good example of the ill effect of his secretiveness was the mutinous attitude of many of the leaders of the Texas army during the famous retreat prior to the battle of San Jacinto. None of them knew certainly what Houston planned to do. He himself has said of that time that he took no counsel in the matter, and that all the blame or all the praise belonged to himself alone. Another characteristic that stirred up animosity was the fact that, when aroused, Houston was never chary of the use of stinging, often humiliating, invectives.

His secretive nature, together with his eloquent, stinging tongue, often brought the man into bitter quarrels. Moreover, the age in which he lived was that in which the practice of duelling flourished. It was considered a gentleman's recourse for redress of wounded honor or offended dignity. It is little wonder, then, that throughout Houston's entire life he was constantly receiving challenges from offended gentlemen who wished redress for real or imaginary wrongs. So far as we have record, however, he never fought but one duel, if we except the Stanbery affair. This one duel that he fought was when he was a young man in Tennessee, and his opponent was General William A. White, another lawyer, and a veteran of the battle of New Orleans. It happened that in this affair Houston had no particular quarrel with White, but White had meddled in

another "affair of honor" that Houston was apparently dodg-
ing so he found himself compelled to offer Houston a challenge
on his own account. It was accepted and the duel was fought;
White was seriously wounded. But Houston took no satisfaction in the outcome, and many times later in his career he denounced the custom of "murder in the attempt to clean up an
injured dignity." Immediately after the affair with White,
he was forced to speak at a political meeting. A friend in intro-
ducing him to his audience referred with heroic allusion to the
duel, but Houston immediately silenced the rising applause by
raising his hand and saying: "My friends, I am greatly opposed
to the practice of duelling, and I decline to be honored as a
duelist. Thank God, that my adversary was no worse injured."
And the man meant what he said.

The duelling pistols shown in the picture were a gift to Houston from the people of Cincinnati, sent on the eve of the battle
of San Jacinto. At the same time these people sent as a gift
to the Texas people the two cannon which are known in Texas
as the "Twin Sisters." The cannon arrived in time for good
service at San Jacinto, but, for some reason, the pistols were
delayed in transit and did not arrive until the victory had been
won. Many times in subsequent years Houston had opportunity to test the efficiency of the weapons, but we have no record
that they were ever used in a duel, for Houston became an
expert in turning challenges aside, either with a humorous
reply or with a straightforward answer that left the challenger no
recourse except a peaceful acceptance of a closed issue. Three
examples of such refusals will suffice to prove the statement:

In the early days of the republic an official beneath Houston
in rank and position challenged him to a duel. Houston's
answer to the bearer of the challenge was evasive, but tart.
Without opening the "note" he said to the messenger, "Go
tell your friend that Houston never fights down hill."

In 1841, when Houston was a candidate for the presidency
the second time, he and David G. Burnet, who was always his
enemy, carried on an acrimonious newspaper controversy—each
abusing the other without stint. Burnet called Houston "Big
Drunk," "Half-Indian," and many other such names, while
Houston retorted with equally bitter invectives, finally accusing

Burnet of being an "ex-hog-thief." This was too much for Burnet's dignity to stand; so he sent Branch T. Archer to challenge Houston to a duel. After Archer's statement of his errand Houston asked: "Upon what does he predicate his demand?" Archer replied it was because Houston had abused Burnet beyond forbearance; to which Houston answered: "Hasn't he abused me to an equal degree? He has done so publicly and privately until I am constrained to believe that the people of Texas are thoroughly disgusted with both of us." The sincerity and stately dignity with which Houston made this reply were far more impressive than the words themselves, and Dr. Archer took the challenge back to Burnet unopened. To the credit of both Burnet and Houston, the matter was dropped.

The third instance that we shall note gave Houston greater pause. The challenge came from Albert Sidney Johnston, and Johnston had good cause to be offended. When the messenger arrived with the challenge, Houston was sitting in his office with his private secretary, Washington D. Miller. After Johnston's friend had stated his business, Houston remained silent for several minutes; then with a sigh he turned to his secretary, saying: "Miller, please see that this challenge is filed in its proper place; it is number sixteen." Turning to the messenger, he said in a polite, kindly tone: "Go, tell your friend that angry gentlemen must await their turn if they duel with me, and say that there are fifteen ahead of him." Before Houston and Johnston met, the cause for discord between them had been cleared away, and they met as friends.

Because of his many refusals to fight duels, some of Houston's enemies called him a coward, but this calumny never made much headway because the man's courage was too well known; not even his challengers ever believed that a sense of fear kept Houston from fighting duels.

The Nibbs home on Oyster Creek, near Sugarland, Texas,
often visited by Houston. He bought his horse from Mrs.
Nibbs enroute to the San Jacinto battlefield.

Collection of Mrs. Lula B. Roberts of Houston

THE NIBBS HOME NEAR SUGAR LAND

HOUSTON was a hospitable man. His home was ever open for the entertainment of his associates, and in turn, he loved to visit his friends. There were many homes in Texas in which he felt perfect freedom. One such, which is of especial interest, was the home of Willis Nibbs, who was William Barrett Travis' law partner at the time of the tragic death of the latter at the Alamo. While on his famous retreat, just before the battle of San Jacinto, Houston spent the night at the home of his friend Nibbs. Next morning he espied a fine white stallion in the corral, and he asked to buy the animal. Nibbs protested, saying that the horse belonged to his wife, whereupon Houston passed the request on to the rightful owner. In her enthusiasm for the Texan cause, Mrs. Nibbs consented to sell the animal, and the price was set at $300; the General gave his personal note therefor and rode proudly away on the beautiful beast. When Houston led the charge at San Jacinto, this horse was shot dead from under him at the time he was severely wounded.

Willis Nibbs did not live long after Texas had become a republic. After living in widowhood for several years, Mrs. Nibbs married Judge Buckley, another of Houston's staunch friends; so the general's visits in this attractive home were never discontinued throughout his life. The old Nibbs-Buckley plantation home still stands on Oyster Creek near Sugar Land and is a fine relic of the days of the Texas Republic.

The First Church of Cedar Bayou, Texas, in which was held a Fourth of July-meeting. A barbecue was included. President Houston was present. Collection of Mrs. B.F. Devereux, Cedar Bayou.

The Church at Cedar Bayou

CEDAR BAYOU runs adjacent to Goose Creek, a tributary to Galveston Bay. Along this waterway settlers established their farm homes during the colonial period of Texas history, and the little log house that they built as a place of worship was one of the first Protestant churches to be erected in Texas. Tradesmen and a few farmers built their homes about the church, and, in time, it became the nucleus of a thriving village. Ten miles from the town of Cedar Bayou there is a point of land extending far into the bay that is known as Cedar Point. In 1841, Houston bought this tract of land, and, on the projection that reached farthest into the bay, he established a simple summer home to which he brought his family every summer to enjoy the cool sea-breezes and long swims in the healthful salt waters.

Through the early 1840's the burning question in Texas was that of annexation to the United States. One of the most famous public discussions of this topic took place at a Fourth of July celebration that was held at the Cedar Bayou church. For this occasion the citizens of the place had prepared for a big barbecue and public speaking, a very popular type of gathering in those times. All the notables for miles around were invited to the affair. Sam Houston and his guest, Andrew Jackson Donelson, who a few months later became the United States minister to the Texas Republic, were there; Mirabeau B. Lamar was there, as well as a score of other celebrities of the new nation. Houston, Lamar, and Donelson all made speeches on the great topic of the day. The people were especially interested in Donelson's speech, not only because he was an eloquent speaker, but also because he was the adopted son of Andrew Jackson and was supposed to speak the opinions of Jackson himself on the subject. But the master of ceremonies, and really the speaker of the day, was Judge Nimrod, of Chappell Hill. He was a highly educated man in his full prime, and John W. Lockhart, in his *Sixty Years on the Brazos*, says: "On this occasion the Judge was full of pluck and in full feather. He soon left the earth and was among the planets on the track of the American Eagle. But the national bird led him from star to star, but wandered most gloriously in the constellation of the original Thirteen, where he wished to plant the Lone Star of Texas. When he began his descent he circled gently among murky clouds, touching now and then a high point, until to his great delight and safety he reached the arc of a rainbow, and after decanting eloquently on its beauties, he slid gracefully to earth again without having rumpled a feather." This is a humorous but excellent description of the kind of speeches made on such occasions in the early days.

The old church where this great political speaking was held is still standing, but it has undergone so many alterations and has had so many additions that there is little resemblance between the building that stands today and the little log house in which the celebration of 1844 was held. Our picture, however, shows the church as it was in Houston's day.

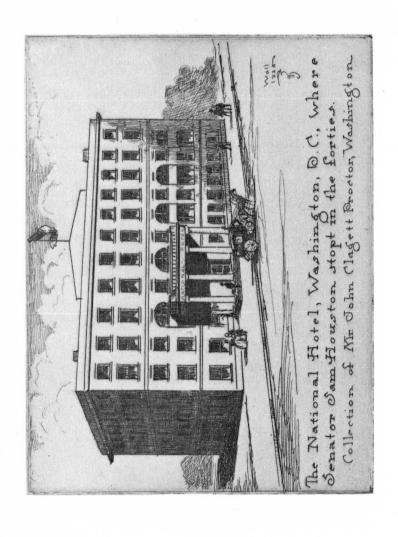

The National Hotel, Washington, D.C., where Senator Sam Houston stopt in the forties. Collection of Mr. John Clagett Proctor, Washington

The National Hotel at Washington, D. C.

E HAVE mentioned in a previous sketch that as early as November, 1836, President Houston had instructed William H. Wharton, the Texan Chargé d'Affaires at Washington, to make an effort to secure annexation as well as recognition of Texas. Wharton did the best he could to carry out instructions, but nothing except recognition was granted in Jackson's administration. Van Buren became president in March, 1837, and in August of that year, Memucan Hunt, then the Texan minister at Washington, again presented proposals for annexation. On account, however, of the "furious opposition of the free states," and the fear that annexation might involve the United States in war with Mexico, the new President refused assent to the proposal. Nevertheless, the application for annexation remained open until Houston ordered its withdrawal in October, 1838. From that time, Texas turned its efforts to securing recognition from Europe. Lamar became president in December, 1838, and in his inaugural speech he declared strongly against annexation, a policy in which he was sustained by an almost unanimous vote of the Congress. The subject was not brought forward again until 1842, when Houston was again president. He then instructed Isaac Van Zandt, Chargé d' Affaires at Washington, to investigate the sentiment of the Congress, and of the people of the United States, relative to the old subject of annexation. But the United States remained hostile—at least indifferent—to the matter until after Texas had secured a truce with Mexico in the summer of 1843, through the good offices of the British and French ministers in Mexico. After this success, Anson Jones, Texan Secretary of State, instructed Van Zandt to state formally to the Washington government that "the subject of annexation was no longer open for discussion." In the words of Jones himself, "This aroused all the dormant jealousies and fears of the United States, and the apathy of the seven years' sleep over the question was shaken off and a treaty of annexation was proposed to be celebrated." The United States had heard rumors that the British were using their influence to abolish slavery in Texas, and decided to forestall such an event by a treaty of annexation; so negotiations for such a treaty were opened, October 16, 1843. But Houston was now the indifferent one. He did not believe that the treaty would pass the Senate of the United States, and if it should not, Texas would be left in a worse condition than ever. And just as Houston had predicted, the treaty was rejected, June, 1844, by a vote of thirty-five to sixteen. After the death of Upshur, United States Secretary of State, John C. Calhoun was appointed to fill the vacancy in the cabinet. He was by this time the leader of the slave states and could not bear to see Texas lost to slavery; consequently he was a strong advocate for annexation. He proposed to carry the measure through the United States Congress in the form of a joint resolution which would require only a majority vote in each house. After a good deal of wrangling and wire-pulling, the American House of Representatives, on February 25, 1845, passed a bill that provided for the annexation of Texas; the Senate passed the bill on March 1, and President Tyler signed it before he left the presidential chair. On October 13 of the same year, the people of Texas ratified this bill almost unanimously and adopted a constitution that had been prepared by their representatives in a convention. President Anson Jones, in turning the archives of the Republic into the hands of James Pinckney Henderson, the first governor of the state of Texas, ended his speech by saying: "Thus a government is changed both in its offices and in its organization, not by violence and disorder, but by the deliberate and free consent of its citizens. . . .The first act of the great drama is now performed. The Republic of Texas is no more."

Sam Houston and Thomas Jefferson Rusk were sent by the new state to represent it in the United States Senate. We can imagine what must have been the feelings of Houston—now fifty-two years old—as he took his seat in that august body. Pilloried in the House of Representatives in 1832, he was now an honored member of the higher chamber. During the first years of his life in Washington as a senator from Texas, he made his home in the National Hotel.

Home of General Sam Houston at Huntsville, Texas, now a Texan Shrine. The General sold this home just before the Civil War began.

Collection of Temple Houston Morrow, Esq., Dallas

SAM HOUSTON'S HOME AT HUNTSVILLE

HORTLY after Houston was elected President of the Republic of Texas for the second time, he bought a tract of land near Huntsville, in Walker county, on which he established his home. There the family lived for nearly twenty years, and there four of his eight children were born. This was the home that Houston always designated as his residence while he was serving in the United States Senate. Always as soon as the senate sessions had adjourned, he hurried back to Texas to rest with his family about him in this Huntsville home, for he loved this place better than any other he possessed.

The house was well located, and Houston always said that it reminded him of his childhood home in Virginia. In 1928, an old lady who had known the place while Houston lived in it, and who had herself lived in the house at a later time, wrote to her granddaughter a description of this Huntsville home of the Houstons. The following description is from her letter: "A picket fence enclosed the large yard, and the front gate which was on the north side, opened on a broad walk leading to the house. Along the front fence, on both sides, were wide beds of roses, lilacs, and flags—white and blue—while on either side of the walk were two large plats with walks between them. Crepe Myrtle trees grew at all four corners of each plat, sixteen trees in all, and when they were in bloom, they filled the whole place with their fragrance. In the centers of these four plats were roses of various hues, lilacs, and syringas, while in beds closely bordering the walk there were narcussus, johnquils, and Easter lilies.

"Three broad steps led to the entrance hall. On the left as one entered the hall, there was a door that led into Mrs. Houston's room, while adjoining her room, there was a small one on the south that her mother occupied. On the right side of the hall, opposite to Mrs. Houston's room, a door opened into the parlor, and back of the parlor, was the girl's room. The hall extended straight through the house to a large back porch, at the west end of which was a large room, usually called the boys' room. I do not remember who occupied the other rooms of the house.

"The back yard, where the kitchen stood, separated from the house by only a short distance, was filled with fruit trees, quince, apple, peach, and fig, while a large pecan tree grew near the back door."

Houston died at Huntsville, but at the time of his death, the family did not live at this home that he loved so well. Just before taking office as governor of Texas in 1859, he had sold it from financial necessity, and he was never able to induce the purchaser to sell it to him again after he retired to private life in 1861. Since, however, he had made it his favorite home for twenty years, the people of Texas have come to associate this place with the home life of the great Texan, and they have selected it as a shrine, dedicated to the memory of Houston. It stands today restored to a semblance of its condition when it was occupied by the Houston family.

Sam Houston's Law Office, Huntsville, Texas.
Collection of The Kinkaid School, Houston, Texas.

Wall
1926

Houston's Law Office at Huntsville

N THE northeast corner of the front yard of Houston's home at Huntsville stands the general's law office. It is a simple log hut, not unlike the one in which he had set up his first law office at Gallatin, Tennessee. Its one door opened on the south, while on the west side of the door grew Houston's favorite rose. It was a multiflora rose of the climbing type, and it covered half of the front of the small log house. In springtime its great clusters of delicate pink flowers filled the entire northeast corner of the yard with a soft fragrance. It was in this log hut that Houston met hundreds of men from all over Texas, and from other parts of the world besides. They came to him, men of high and low degree, for legal advice, for conferences on the leading issues of the day, or merely for companionship and friendly intercourse. All were welcome; and Houston gave advice, discussed the destiny of a nation, or cracked a joke with equal facility and enjoyment. Happy and discerning was the thought that led the people of Texas to preserve these simple, homelike buildings at Huntsville as a Houston shrine.

Old Willard Hotel, Washington, D.C., where Senator Houston stopt at the end of his term.

Collection of Mr. John Clagett Proctor, Washington, D.C.

The Old Willard Hotel at Washington, D. C.

URING the 1850's Houston made the Willard Hotel his home while he was at Washington. These last years of his service in the Senate were years of turmoil. The whole nation was in the throes of sectional agitation. Party alignments were breaking down; old parties were passing away or were being rendered impotent by internal factions; new parties, some secret and short-lived, were springing up. Throughout it all, Houston remained a staunch Union man. In his earliest political experiences he had learned, from his old mentor and chief, the motto, "*The Union, it must be preserved.*" This was still the central theme of his political creed, and the widening gulf between the North and the South gave him great concern and sorrow. As time went on, he heard the cry of "secession" grow stronger and stronger in the sections which feared that their rights and their sovereignty were being crushed into oblivion. Houston felt that if the Union were dissolved, his life work would have been in vain, for since 1830 he had been obsessed with the idea of Texan independence and annexation—union with the United States. Now, if disunion came, could Texas stand alone?

It was largely because of his dread, his fear of disunion, that Houston allowed himself to be drawn into the American party (Know-Nothing party), whose key principle was maintenance of the Union. He had hoped that this new party could develop sufficient importance and strength to divert the mind of the nation from the ever more dangerous subject of slavery. But the party was secret in much of its policy, and it soon lost favor everywhere. Houston's alignment with it made him unpopular, even in Texas. Many of his staunchest friends and supporters deserted him, and in 1858, he found himself defeated for re-election to the United States Senate.

But during his twelve years of service in the national forum, Houston had played no mean part in its deliberations. He had been one of the leaders in the Oregon controversy; in 1850 he had supported Clay in debate and had voted with him on the Compromise Bill; and he had opposed with strong feeling the

Kansas and Nebraska Bill. In his speech on this bill he said: "Sir, if this repeal [of the Missouri Compromise] takes place, I shall have seen the commencement of this agitation, but the youngest child now born will not live to see its termination." And his foresight was keen and clear.

Fort Worth, Texas, where Sam Houston visited in the Summer of the campaign of 1857.

Courtesy of Mr. Howard W. Peak, Fort Worth.

Fort Worth in 1857

N THE preceding sketch, mention was made of the fact that in 1859 Houston was defeated for re-election to the United States Senate. He had lost popularity in Texas because of his alignment with the American party, and because he had voted against the Kansas-Nebraska Bill, which declared the Missouri Compromise of 1820 "inoperative and void" and permitted slave owners to carry their slaves into that territory. Houston made a speech in the Senate against this bill, in which he elaborated the reasons for his vote against the measure, his most potent argument being that it was his firm conviction that Nature herself had already prohibited slavery from the northern territory, and that any attempt to establish it in Kansas or Nebraska would prove futile and serve only to alienate further the quarreling sections. His foresight concerning the matter, as we know, was prophetic; but his arguments fell on deaf ears in Texas, because the people, for the most part, were already prejudiced on the subject of slavery. But probably the strongest reason why Houston's popularity in the state had waned was that he had been out of the state for the greater part of every year for a whole decade, and he had lost personal touch with the masses.

No one understood the danger of this handicap better than he himself did. He decided that a close understanding with the people themselves could be re-established more quickly and more effectively by a term in the governor's chair than by any other means; consequently, he announced that he would be a candidate for that office in the election of 1857. Perhaps there were other reasons for his decision. He was an astute politician; he may have decided to put his popularity to the test before the time for his campaign in 1858 for a return to the United State Senate. Whatever was in his mind, he made the campaign for election as governor in 1857. His opponent was Hardin R. Runnels, a Mississippi planter who had removed to Texas with his slaves in 1841 and had settled in Bowie county. From 1847 to 1855 he had represented Bowie county in the Texas legislature, and he had served as speaker of the house in

1853-1854. In 1855 he was made lieutenant governor and served in that office during Governor Pease's second administration.

Houston campaigned under difficulties. As we have said, he had been out of the state for ten years and did not personally know the majority of the voters as he had once done; moreover, he had only recently returned to the Democratic party and was under the necessity of explaining to dull ears his deflection from the Democratic fold. There was yet another difficulty that he had to surmount. He had always had strong political enemies within the state as well as staunch friends; his conduct in becoming a member of the American party and his vote against the Kansas-Nebraska Bill had, to use his own words, "given the enemies plenty of political thunder, and they had not failed to crack down with their big guns." The result of the campaign, therefore, was a vote of 32,552 to 23,628, a majority of 8,924 in Runnels's favor.

Despite his handicaps, however, Houston had made no mean race. He had traversed the greater part of Texas, he had made speeches in nearly all sections of the state, and he had met as man to man the generation of young voters to whom Sam Houston had been but a name and a tradition before this time. While he was campaigning in East Texas, he went out to the new frontier town of Fort Worth—at the time little more than a military camp against hostile Indians—and made a speech. Houston did not hope to gain many votes in this sparsely settled frontier district, but it gave him touch with a number of young men; moreover, he said that he had a sentimental reason—he wished "to raise his voice in blessing over the settlement that had been named in honor of his old friend and companion-in-arms, William Worth."

Judge Williamson's home, three miles from Marshall, Texas, where General Houston often visited

Photo by Miss Natalie Williams, Marshall, Texas.

THE HOME OF JUDGE JOHN H. WILLIAMSON, MARSHALL, TEXAS

DURING the campaigns of 1857 and 1859 Houston made many speeches in East Texas. He had lost touch with the people in this section even more than in the central and the western parts of the state; moreover, he had many enemies in this eastern section. But he had many friends there, too, and no more loyal one than Judge John H. Williamson of Marshall. Judge Williamson was born and educated in Philadelphia, Pennsylvania. In 1849 he started west to join the gold rush to California, but when an accident on the way caused him to change his mind, he came to Texas instead. He was just past his thirtieth birthday, well educated in both the liberal subjects and the law. Upon his arrival, however, his funds were exhausted; so he decided to teach school in order to get enough money to set up a law office. In 1849-1852 he taught the school at Elysian Fields, but in the late summer of 1852 he moved to Marshall, opened a law office, and practiced there until the year of his death. For six years of that time he served as district judge of that section, and for six years he was the judge of Harrison county, making a service of twelve years on the bench. From the time of his arrival in Texas he was a political friend of Houston, and during the campaigns of 1857 and 1859 he was very active in the general's behalf. During Houston's work in East Texas, in these campaigns, he and his workers were frequently entertained at Judge Williamson's home three miles from Marshall.

The Tree, under which spoke Senator Sam Houston, at Marshall, Texas, in the Spring, 1849.

Photo by Miss Natalie Williams, Marshall

The Houston Tree at Marshall, Texas

VER since Joyce Kilmer wrote his beautiful poem, *Trees*, the whole world has been given a deeper reverence for noble trees. Throughout our nation there are many trees that have become as individual as human beings, because we have associated them with events of moment that occurred beneath their branches. In our own state of Texas there are many trees that should be preserved as monuments to events with which they are concerned, and it is a pleasure to know that our people are beginning to realize the historic value of these silent witnesses of our past. One tree in Marshall, Texas, is now being cared for as though it were a thing of flesh and blood. It is the tree under which Houston stood in 1849 while he made a speech in his campaign for his second term as United States senator; and again in 1857 he spoke to a small group of friends and supporters as they all stood together beneath the shade of this tree. In 1913 the Sesame Club of Marshall placed a brass tablet on this tree as a memorial of the time Sam Houston spoke beneath its branches.

Barnums Hotel, 176 Broadway, New York City, in which
Sam Houston, Senator, lodged in the fifties.
Collection of New York Historical Society, N.Y.C.

Barnum Hotel, New York City

ONE OF Houston's staunchest friends in writing of him once said: "The great difference between both Burnet and Lamar compared with Houston is that both the former were born and reared in the lap of luxury, and for that reason were not used to the inconveniences, hardships and trials of frontier life. They could not stand the shock of severe criticism; it made them nervous and irascible in disposition and caused them to be led into traps set for them by their enemies. Houston, on the other hand, had come up almost from poverty, had been compelled to fight his way to the top, so was able to withstand criticism so bitter and unfeeling that it would have crushed the heart of a more sensitive man. Houston, however, no more felt the sting and bitterness of the enemy darts than a rhinoceros would feel the blows from a boy's pop gun. Taunts and criticism that pierced the very vitals of his enemies fell off Houston, and, as if by magic, returned like boomerangs, to inflict fatal wounds on the thrower. And it was well known that whenever he desired Houston could crush his opponents . . . ." After his defeat in 1857, he himself wrote to his wife: "My dear, I regret the bitterness of this campaign for your sake. I know that all these things that are being said about me wound your tender heart. But you must not let them worry you. None of them are wholly true, and more than half have no germ of truth whatever. For myself, I do not mind what my enemies may say; their dirty scandal falls off me like water off a duck's back."

It was in this spirit that Houston returned to Washington in 1858, well assured in his own mind that the next year and a half would be his last service in the United States Senate. Moreover, another sorrow weighed on his mind and spirit. In 1857 his old friend and senate-mate, Thomas J. Rusk, had, in a fit of mental depression, taken his own life. Houston missed Rusk more than the world will ever know.

At this time, however, an old dream that haunted the man throughout his life again filled his sleeping and waking hours.

Once while he was still a young man and serving as the governor of Tennessee, it had been rumored in political circles throughout the nation that Jackson, then the President of the United States, had slated Houston for his successor, and was secretly coaching the young man for the position. The break in his domestic life and his subsequent exile among the Indians had been a rude awakening from this dream of his youth. He turned his hopes and plans in another direction, and forgot it. In 1855-1856 it appeared again to haunt him, for in that year prospects looked bright for him to be nominated for the presidency on the American ticket; but a cog slipped in the political machinery, and again the dream vanished. Still again in 1859, although his own Texas had refused to elect him for a third term to the Senate, out in the nation there were many who believed that he was the only man in the United States in whom the Democrats could hope to hold both the northern and the southern factions of their party together; so his chance for nomination as a candidate for the presidency again seemed bright for a moment. But various manipulations of politics played him an evil trick, and he was not able to surmount the hindrances and the mighty combination against him. He had done what he could, however, to make the dream of his life come true, before it vanished forever.

With this hope of winning, at last, the desire of his life, it is not surprising to find that Houston made frequent trips to New York, Philadelphia, Boston, and other cities, where he made speeches on various subjects. While in New York during these late years of the fifties, he made the Barnum—later known as the Howard—Hotel his headquarters. Where he lived while he was in the other cities we do not know.

"Ashland," Henry Clay's home, Lexington, Kentucky.
Sam Houston attended Clay's funeral, 1852.

Ashland—the Home of Henry Clay

AM HOUSTON and Henry Clay were alike in at least two respects. Both men consistently and persistently fought with all the powers of their statesmanship for the preservation of the Union, and both sorrowed to see the Union rent asunder by the heat of unthinking passion. Then, too, the life ambition of both men was to be President of the United States, but neither reached the goal of his highest hope. In most other respects these two famous sons of the Old Dominion State were vastly different; nor were they always friends. As a disciple of Jackson, Houston used his powers to checkmate the ambitions of Clay through many years; but when the storm clouds of the fifties began to lower, and threats of disunion began to be breathed into public discussions and debates, Clay and Houston forgot their old hatreds and supported each other in a great effort for future peace. None knew better than they the blight that internecine war would cast upon their beloved country. In this respect, Houston lived to see his worst fears realized, but Clay died in 1852.

As a member of the Congressional commission Houston attended Clay's funeral, held at "Ashland," the beautiful Lexington home of the "Great Pacificator," and none can doubt that the tears which fell from Houston's eyes upon the bier of his erstwhile enemy were marks of real grief. A great man had gone; a mighty co-worker in the noble effort to preserve the Union had been forced to lay down the task before the work had well begun.

The Capitol, Austin, connected with General Houston's activities while Governor from 1859 to 1861.

Collection of Kinkaid School, Houston.

The State Capitol at Austin in 1859

T HAS been mentioned in another sketch that Houston's burning desire to preserve the Union had led him to become allied, for a few years, with the American (the Know-Nothing) party, a political party that was short-lived, and always unpopular in Texas. By this alignment he had lost the confidence and support of many of his staunchest old friends and supporters, and consequently, in 1858, he was defeated for a third term in the United States Senate. His senatorial career ended on March 4, 1859. Ere this, however, even as early as 1857, he had seen that his best efforts to serve Texas, and his greatest hope of holding his state to a firm allegiance to the federal Union, would depend upon his becoming the chief executive of the state government; therefore, in 1857 he became a candidate for the governorship. He was defeated in the race by Hardin R. Runnels. This was a blow that would have severely smitten a less brave, a less unselfish man—the humiliation of being twice repudiated by his people within the space of less than two years. But Houston never lost confidence in the basic good-sense of the Texas people, nor in their ultimate loyalty to him. These defeats merely proved to him that his long absence from constant personal touch with the masses in Texas had given his political enemies ample opportunity to spread evil propaganda against him, in order to promote their own ambitious interests. He realized, also, that his alliance with the American party had been a political mistake, although his reasons for making the connection had been for what he considered the ultimate good of the whole nation.

So, nothing daunted by defeat, Houston decided to put his popularity in Texas to the severest test. In 1859 he again offered himself a candidate for the governor's office, and against Runnels, the very man who had defeated him by a large majority in 1857. The returns of the 1859 election were the reverse of those two years before. Houston won the office by a large majority and once more became the chief executive of Texas, this time, however, with the title of governor of a state, instead of president of an independent nation.

During his fourteen years of absence from state politics many changes had been wrought, no more striking evidence of which was manifested than in the better housing facilities for the government. On Capitol Hill at Austin stood a stone building that compared favorably with the state capitols of the day, while the mansion for the governor's family was as elegant in all of its appointments as the governor's house of any of the other Southern states.

But Houston's administration was not destined for quietude or peace. Probably Houston had not dared to hope for such a bright future. We may be sure, though, that he was determined to use all the powers of his mind and personality in an effort to hold Texas in the Union; but even this effort was to prove a hopeless task. Lincoln was elected President of the United States in November, 1860; in Texas, on February 23, 1861, the people, through delegates met in convention, voted to secede from the federal Union and to join the Confederacy of the Southern, slave-holding states. And the state legislature declared the decision as binding as any law of the land.

Governor's Mansion, Austin, Texas, where lived Sam
Houston while Governor, 1859-1861.
Collection of Mrs. Rogers Kelley, Edinburg, Texas.

The Governor's Mansion at Austin

URING Houston's short term of office as governor of Texas, he and his family occupied the governor's mansion, the same that is still the home of all the Texas governors while they are in office. This stately old house, built in the Southern colonial style, was erected in 1854. When the Houstons went to live in the "Mansion," they carried with them a family of seven gaily happy children: Samuel, Jr., Nannie Elizabeth, Margaret Lea, Mary Willie, Antoinette Power, Andrew Jackson, and William Rogers. And there, in August, 1860, the last of the Houston children, Temple Lea, was born. These children filled the house with laughter and the joyousness of youth. Never before, nor since, has the governor's home sheltered so large a family. But clouds of war and premonitions of disaster soon dispelled the lightness even of childish laughter in the governor's house, for the subjects of conversation which they heard in the drawing room, and often in the family circle, were concerned mostly with the seriousness of affairs, or how disaster might possibly be averted.

After Texas had voted for secession, and had joined the Confederacy, Governor Houston was asked to take the oath of allegiance to the Confederate government. His refusal to take this oath was the cause of his removal from office on March 18, 1861. This act closed the public career of Sam Houston.

On the night of March 19, 1861, a few close friends of the governor's family were gathered at the "Mansion" on a purely friendly visit, to express their fidelity and friendship for the Houstons. Mrs. Houston was hurrying preparations for leaving Austin to retire to their own home. Just before the clock struck nine, messengers arrived to tell the governor that an armed group were ready and waiting for his word to begin the business of reinstating him in his office. Houston was amazed at their statements, and he made to them the following reply: "My God! Is it possible that all the people have gone mad? Is it possible that my friends are willing to inaugurate a war that would be more horrible than the one inaugurated by the secessionists? Do you know, my friends, that this civil war that is now beginning will be as horrible as his Satanic Majesty could desire? And would you be willing to deluge the capital of Texas with the blood of Texans merely to keep one poor old man in a high position for a few days longer—in a position that belongs to the people? No—No! Go tell my deluded friends that I am proud of their friendship, proud of their love and loyalty. I hope that I may always retain both. But say to them that I beg for the sake of humanity and of justice that they disperse, that they go to their homes and conceal from the world that they would have been guilty of such an act."

Some weeks later Lincoln offered Houston a commission as major general in the United States army. It was declined. Houston was not a Lincoln man; he had always blamed Lincoln for much of the trouble that had been stirred up during the fifties, and he readily conceded that Lincoln's election to the presidency was a national calamity, for Lincoln was the candidate of a mere sectional party. But he persistently argued that Lincoln's election was not a just cause for secession until the man had had a chance to show whether or not he would act as the nation's chief, or as the mere tool of a partisan, sectional group. If the latter course should be pursued by the new President, that would be time for secession, for secession under such circumstances would be the only recourse. Until that time, however, all citizens of every state should rest secure in the Constitution, for the Constitution was not dead, nor had it been annulled by Lincoln's election.

Woodlawn, home of Ex-Gov. E. M. Pease, Austin, Texas, Houston and Pease were close political friends. Collection of Mr. R. Niles Graham, Austin

Wall 1935

Woodlawn, the Home of Governor E. M. Pease

OUR artist has presented in this group of pictures an attractive etching of "Woodlawn," the beautiful home of Ex-Governor E. M. Pease, and while no historical, or traditional, evidence can be found to prove that Houston was ever a visitor in this home, logical inference leads one to believe that he may have sat there for many a quiet hour of conference with its master during the troubled times of 1860 and 1861. In the first place, Houston and Pease had been friends since 1835, and at only one period during this time (1854-1857) had there been a coolness in their feelings. In 1860-1861 both men took the same high ground concerning the preservation of the Union and concerning the secession question; so it is very probable that Houston often visited Woodlawn. For where could he and Governor Pease find greater security from interruption than in the heart of Pease's own home? But whether or not Houston was ever within the doors of Woodlawn, there are other reasons that may justify this sketch.

Woodlawn is perhaps the most nearly perfect example in Texas of the Southern colonial type of architecture, and because of the good taste, or the family sentiment, of its owners, it has escaped the modern innovations that so many of the beautiful old Southern homes have suffered. In Austin, this beautiful old house is commonly spoken of as the "Pease Home," and indeed it has been the property of the Pease family for some seventy-five years, but it was built for James B. Shaw, a cultured young Irishman, who had immigrated to Texas in 1837. Shaw was of gentle birth and had had the best of educational advantages in both Ireland and England, but the hopelessness of political preferment in his fatherland, added to an adventurous nature, led him to seek his fortune in America. He landed in New Orleans, where he set up in business and remained for a year and a half before the tales of excitement in Texas "caused him to lose his better judgment" and press on to the West. He had not been in the new republic long before Henry Smith discovered that he was an efficient clerk and of great service in the Treasury Department; and Smith is even known to have admitted that a great part of his own efficiency in the Treasury Department was due to the excellent financial training of young Shaw. But the young man craved adventure, and for almost two years he could not be induced to do the routine of office work; he joined the Texan army as a private and was sure to be one of the foremost in the various Indian campaigns of the times. In 1840, however, Lamar appointed him comptroller, and from that time until 1858 he was constantly in public service in one position or another. He was a great admirer and staunch friend of Houston, and throughout Houston's second term as president of the republic, Shaw was one of his most trusted advisers concerning financial matters.

During his early stay in that city, as well as during many subsequent visits, "young Jim Shaw" had wooed and won the heart and hand of one of the most beautiful and popular women in New Orleans. Together the young people planned their future home which was to be at Austin, Texas. To this end Shaw bought about two hundred acres of land lying along Shoal Creek, just on the outskirts of the new capital, and during 1852-1853, Captain Abraham Cook, a master-builder of the time, constructed beautiful "Woodlawn" according to specifications drawn up by Shaw and the fair one of New Orleans. Before the date set for the wedding, however, the young woman proved false to her promise and married another man. Though the jilted lover was heartbroken for a time, with true Irish impetuosity he soon found consolation in another fair face, and in less than six months from the time he should have been married to his faithless sweetheart, he married another and carried his bride to Woodlawn as its mistress. But fate was frowning on James Shaw. In less than two years the little child that was born to the young couple lay buried in the garden of the beautiful mansion, and a few months later the mother followed her babe in death. It is said that James Shaw would never enter the doors of Woodlawn after he had laid his young wife to rest at Oakwood. He felt that the place held for him a spell of trouble and disaster; so it was locked up and advertised for sale. On July 25, 1859, it was sold to Elisha M. Pease.

Elisha Marshall Pease was another public servant who had proved himself of great usefulness to Texas. Born at Enfield, Connecticut, January 3, 1812, he received an elementary education at the Westfield Academy, not far from his home. At the age of fourteen he left school to become a clerk in a country store. In 1834 business for his firm carried him to New Orleans, and while there he heard a great deal of interesting talk concerning Texas. Having decided to investigate the situation for himself, he took a boat which landed him at Velasco during the early days of 1835. He went from Velasco to Bastrop, (Mina) where he became a clerk and a student in the law office of Don Carlos Barrett. In the late summer of the same year he was appointed secretary to the Committee of Safety of Mina. This was his first public office in Texas. But events moved swiftly towards revolution in Texas during the summer and fall of 1835, and young Pease joined the company of R. M. Coleman when it was raised. As a member of that company he participated in the first clash at Gonzales on October 2, 1835. As soon as the provisional government was ready to function, however, he was appointed, through the influence of D. C. Barrett, to the office of secretary of the provisional council, a position he held until March 1, 1836. Although not a delegate to the convention of March, 1836, he was at Washington while that body was in session, and he had a large part in the formation of both the Texan Declaration of Independence and the constitution for the new republic. His name, however, does not appear as a signer of either document since he was not an official member of the convention. During the summer of 1836 he served successively as chief clerk of the navy and the treasury departments, and after the death of Secretary Hardiman he was Acting Secretary of the Treasury. In November, 1836, he was appointed clerk of the judiciary committee of the House, and in that capacity he drafted laws creating and defining the duties of various county officers. In December, 1836, Houston, who had been his friend from the time of his arrival in the territory, offered him the portfolio of Postmaster General, but the young man declined the office, preferring to continue his law studies in the office of John A. Wharton at Brazoria. There he was admitted to the bar in April, 1837, and almost immediately was appointed comptroller of public accounts. He accepted the position, but he resigned in the following December to become a law partner with John A. Wharton and John W. Harris. After Wharton's death the Harris and Pease partnership continued for many years.

But while a successful career as a lawyer was adding to the young man's fame, he was seldom without a public office. He served in the Texas Congress, first as a representative, then as a senator. In both houses he rendered valuable service in formulating laws that regulated the procedure of district courts and organized probate rules, as well as many other judicial measures. In 1853, and again in 1855, he was elected governor of the state. During his gubernatorial terms, the revolutionary debt was finally cancelled, a public school fund of two million dollars was created, and alternate sections of land granted to railroads under the old charters were set apart for public schools; asylums for the lunatic, the deaf and dumb, the blind, and the orphans were established with ample grants of land for their support, and $100,000 was set aside as a nucleus for the establishment of a state university. All these measures were recommended by Governor Pease and carried out largely through his leadership.

Up to 1860-1861, Governor Pease had always acted with the Democratic party in Texas, but when the question of secession shook the state's foundations, he was found to be anti-secession and anti-Confederacy, and ever afterwards he aligned himself with the Republican party. In opposing secession and the Confederacy he occupied much the same high ground as did General Houston. He did not believe that Lincoln's election was justification for disruption of the Union. Throughout the Civil War he remained in Texas but took no active part in public affairs. In 1867 he was appointed provisional governor by the military authorities and held the position until 1869, when he resigned because he and the military commandant could not agree concerning the reorganization of the state government.

He retired to private life and was one of the organizers of the First National Bank of Austin. As vice president of the institution he took an active interest in its management till the day of his death, August 26, 1883. There was another event of great importance in the man's private life. He was married in 1850 to Miss Lucadia Christiana Niles of Poquonok, Connecticut. For several years after their marriage the couple lived at Brazoria, but upon his election to the governor's office Pease moved his family, his wife and two small daughters to

Austin, where they boarded with Mrs. William Ward, the wife of the commissioner of the general land office. Although Mrs. Pease selected the site and supervised many phases of the construction of the present governor's mansion, she was never its mistress. When Governor Pease purchased Woodlawn, the family immediately occupied the estate and made it the family home. After Governor Pease's death Mrs. Pease continued her residence there until her death in January, 1905. Woodlawn is owned and occupied today by her grandson, Mr. Niles Graham.

So while it is possible that Houston was never in Woodlawn, it was the home of two of his warm personal and political friends, and he may have visited there during Shaw's occupancy as well as during that of Pease. At any rate, it has been the home of two men who loved Texas and who served her interests long and faithfully.

JEFF HAMILTON
SAM HOUSTON'S ONE-TIME SLAVE IN 1934
Photograph by Mrs Temple H. Morrow, Dallas

JEFF HAMILTON, HOUSTON'S OLD SLAVE

IKE many another Southern man, Sam Houston did not believe in the "divine right" of slavery, although he owned several negroes. He accepted the institution as an evil that had been fastened on the South by its climate, by its agricultural pursuits, and by the economic needs of past generations. He verily believed that the institution would die a "natural death" in a few decades if left alone, because it was becoming more and more of a burden and less and less of an economic asset to the sections where it existed. He did not think that the North had any right to meddle in the affair, for they had rid themselves of the institution because it was unprofitable to them, and he thought the South should have the same privilege. He deplored the attitude of the abolitionists of the North; he considered them evil meddlers in the rights of others; but he thought that the Union could be maintained in spite of them and that constitutional adjustments could be made in peace concerning all the questions of the various sections of the Union.

As has already been stated, Houston owned several slaves. One, a very black man, Joshua, was a skilled blacksmith. The general permitted him to have as his own all the money that he was able to make in his idle time. When, in 1864, Mrs. Houston, newly widowed, was having grave difficulties with her financial affairs, Joshua rode up to her house at Independence one day on an old lop-eared mule. He came to the house carrying a leather pouch containing two thousand dollars in gold and silver, and he begged Mrs. Houston to accept the money as a gift from him. Of course this loyalty was very greatly appreciated by the Houston family, but Mrs. Houston would not accept the old man's money. She advised him to spend it in educating his children. This the old negro did. His son, Sam Houston, now an old man, is president of the Sam Houston Normal Training School for Colored People at Huntsville.

But the only person still living who belonged to Houston as a slave is Jeff Hamilton, called "Uncle Jeff" by al Texans from Governor Allred down to the little boys on the street. He lives with his daughter in Belton. He is a hale little fellow and seems to have many more years of life in store for him. He claims that General Houston bought him as a gift for his son, Andrew Jackson Houston. Colonel Andrew Jackson Houston, of LaPorte, Texas, is the only one of Sam Houston's children who is still living.

Sam Houston's home and office, at Liberty
Texas. It has long ago disappeared. It was
photographed by Mr Gus Boettcher.
Collection of Col. A. J. Houston, La Porte, Tex.

Houston's Home at Liberty, Texas

UPON leaving Austin in the spring of 1861, the Houston family soon settled themselves for the summer at their lodge on Cedar Point in Galveston Bay. Houston's life had been filled with storms and tempests. Now nearly seventy, and a man "who had seen about all there was in life to live for"—high honors, high prerogatives, great responsibilities—he hoped to find peace and quiet, real rest from the burdens and cares of public life. He wished to live out the remainder of his days just as a man, as the father of a large family, as a simple farmer of the soil and herdsman of the plains. At least this is the life that Houston said he wished to live and no doubt he really thought that he was in earnest. But he was of the doer type of man, and for nearly seventy years he had lived strenuously from one great plan to another; he had formed deep-set habits of activity. Consequently, a few months of quiet gave the needed rest, and his busy brain was again ready for activities.

Resolutely he turned from the thought of active participation in political affairs to the education of his children and to cordial associations with old and tried friends. And it is of these phases of his life that the remaining sketches will treat.

As has been said, Houston's was an active, restless spirit. He loved change; he loved travel. Almost from the time of his marriage he had set up four homes in Texas, and for a time all four were furnished and ready for the family to move in at any time. It is said that whenever Houston became lonesome or restless at one of these homes he would announce to the family that they would move; he would put Mrs. Houston and the children, and probably a servant, in the great yellow family carriage, drawn by four horses or mules, while he rode ahead on horseback or in a one-horse gig. These movings were not so strenuous a matter as the movings of the average family, for, since the home to which they were going was as fully equipped as the one they were leaving, they had to carry little else besides their clothing. These four homes that are known to have been kept furnished at once were located at Huntsville, at Independence, at Cedar Point, and at Liberty.

Concerning the home at Liberty there is very little known; it seems to have been acquired in trade, on one of the real estate deals that the general was fond of making. It was never a favorite residence with the Houston family, and there is probably not a picture extant of the entire house; however, while the demolition of this old landmark was taking place a few years ago, Mr. Gus Boettcher, a local photographer, took the view of the front porch that is presented here. Efforts to preserve this home of Houston were not successful, because of the lack of funds. A bronze tablet has recently been placed on the site of this Liberty home of the Houston family, but unfortunately it can never help the Texas citizen of the future to visualize the life of the famous man who once lived there as the old house would have done.

Watch worn by General Sam Houston
Collection of Mrs. Wirt Davis, Dallas, Texas.

General Houston's Watch

ENERAL Houston was fond of jewelry and had several watches during his life, but the one pictured here is one that was given him by his brother William when he left Tennessee. It is a silver watch, and was once a good timekeeper; therefore, it was a favorite with the general, who wore it during many years. He finally gave it to a cousin, through whose descendants it came into the possession of the present owners, Mr. and Mrs. Wirt Davis of Dallas.

But this picture has even greater significance for us, because it brings to mind the stories told of Houston's idiosyncrasies in the matter of dress. A close study of the man and of his writings reveals the fact that he looked upon life as a great drama in which a single individual might be called upon to play many roles. At least, this was certainly true of the life of Sam Houston; and it is also true that he loved to dress for the part he was called upon to play. He loved fine materials, and he generally loved for them to be showy, although he had a keen sense of appreciation for the delicate tints of a flower or the sheen on a feather. One of the most beautiful documents from Houston's pen now extant is to be found in the Rosenberg library. It is a brief note, in his own hand, with a beautifully ornate rubric; and this note accompanied the gift of a feather to a lady. The feather was one of great beauty that had been a gift to Houston from young Flacco, the pride of the Lipan tribe. But it would be impossible to relate all the stories showing Houston's love of adornment. A few will suffice to reveal the man's inherent vanity and his consciousness of always playing a part.

This story is told of Houston's dress on the last day of his campaign for the governorship of Tennessee in 1827. The campaign had been a colorful one, the very kind for which Houston was particularly fitted, for log-rolling, barbecues, picnics, and dances were his forte. He closed his canvass at Nashville. "Mounted on a superb dapple-gray horse he came riding unannounced into the midst of a crowd of his constituents. He was the observed of all observers on account of his costume. He wore a bell-crowned beaver hat, standing collar, and patent-leather stock, ruffled lace-trimmed shirt, black satin vest, and shiny black trousers, gathered at the waist with legs full 'the same size from seat to ankle.' In the place of a coat the broad shoulders were loosely draped with a gorgeous Indian hunting shirt, encircled by a beaded red sash with a polished metal clasp. His socks were lavishly embroidered and his pumps were set off by silver buckles." This was, no doubt, Houston's idea of how the aspirant for the governor's seat should dress.

Many accounts are to be found of Houston's appearance at dances or other evening entertainments held in log huts with puncheon floors. Invariably his dress was rich, consisting of velvet suit, fancy and showy waistcoat, and black patent-leather pumps. On his farm, however, he dressed as an ordinary herdsman, and his brogan shoes seldom had strings with which to fasten them. As president of the republic he dressed the part as he thought it should be played, however inappropriate his dress might seem to others. We have the description that Audubon gives of the small two-room log shack, facetiously called the "White House of Texas," to enter which, in wet weather, one must wade in mud and water above the ankles, to find cluttered rooms and muddy floors, but withal, to be greeted by the president dressed in a velvet suit and cravat of cavalier fashion. Then, too, the whole world has heard the story of how the great senator from Texas would wa k the streets of Washington wearing a leopard-skin vest, with a gay Indian blanket drawn close about him instead of the dark coat or cloak usually worn by gentlemen of that day.

As was said above, General Houston was fond of wearing jewelry, and he possessed a fine collection of rings, shirt-studs, and silver and gold mounted walking canes. After receiving the wound in his ankle at San Jacinto, the general was seldom seen without a walking stick, although it seems to have been carried more from force of habit than from need of it. Invariably he wore four, sometimes five, rings on his fingers, and always a watch with a heavy chain dangled across his waistcoat. This love of jewelry was the subject of many jibes on the part of his enemies, as the pages of the newspapers of the 1840's and 1850's will testify. Even his warmest friends disapproved of the general's "decorations," as they were wont to call his jewelry.

Houston was thoroughly aware of the criticism of his taste in dress, and he utterly ignored it. The following story illustrates his attitude concerning the matter: One day, during the fifties, when a group of his friends, mostly younger men, were discussing the general's "Indian love" of showy clothes and jewelry, Houston came near them without being seen. He understood very well what the subject of conversation was and the cause of their mocking laughter, but he met the group with his usual hearty, good-natured greetings. Washington D. Miller, who was sincerely fond of his chief, fearing that the old man might have overheard some of their remarks, and, moreover, wishing to save his companions from embarrassment, said: "General, we were discussing that remarkable carnelian signet that you always wear; it must be a treasured relic." Whereupon, Houston gave interesting stories concerning the rings on his fingers, the studs in his shirt, his watch and chain, and even the silver-headed cane in his hand. Each piece of adornment had its own story, which lost nothing of its interest in the general's telling of it. Finally pointing to a plain gold band on the little finger of his left hand, a band that had become thin from years of wear, he said: "And this ring is my greatest treasure. An old mother placed it on the finger of her wayward son, as a talisman, when the youth left her hut for his first battle-field." By the time Houston had finished telling the history of his jewelry, all the mockery and disapproval of the group had disappeared, and the old man passed on with a chuckle and a smile of cunning amusement at his own sagacity.

While the story of the plain gold ring is an oft-told tale in Texas, it is beautiful and touching enough to bear retelling many times. It runs thus: In his youth Sam Houston was considered a wayward boy by his older brothers and by the more staid heads of the neighborhood. He would not do farm work; he would not be confined in a store; he refused to attend school; he wandered among the Indians. He and his brothers quarreled. But Elizabeth Houston's heart—as mothers' hearts are wont to do—went out in an all-enveloping tenderness for this "queer one" of her flock. Her wayward boy was probably dearer to her than the other more decorous ones; but she was never maudlin in her affections. Her stern old Presbyterian soul demanded righteousness of living and thinking. No doubt, her boy Sam often grieved her heart, but when he enlisted in the army in 1813, she took her saved-up money and bought him two presents. One was a very practical gift, the best musket that she could find, and on presenting it she said: "My son, take this musket and never disgrace it; for remember, I had rather that all my sons should fill one honorable grave, than that one of them should turn his back to save his life. Go, then, and remember, too, that while the door of my cabin is open to brave men, it is eternally shut against cowards." These were stern words, but while she held her son's hand in hers at parting, she tenderly slipped upon his finger a plain gold ring which, she whispered, was to be his talisman in an evil world.

Throughout his life that plain gold ring seldom left Sam Houston's hand; and it is said that at his request his wife, Margaret, slipped it from his finger after she had closed his eyes in death. She turned it slowly so that his children might see the talismanic creed that Elizabeth Houston had said must ever shine in the conduct of her son, and they read the simple word *"Honor."*

Collection of Col. A. J. Houston   La Porte, Texas

A Bust of Houston

IN THE preceding sketch Houston's love of adornment was mentioned. This picture of a life mask, made in 1860 by Henry Dexter of Boston, reminds us of the famous Texan's passion for having his own likeness made. In a collection of Houston's pictures in the archives of the University of Texas, there are copies of more than thirty different pictures of the man, and probably these are only a few of the many that he had made from time to time throughout his life. This bust by Dexter is of especial interest, because it was made near the end of Houston's life and because the artist was one of broad reputation in the world of art. We feel assured, therefore, that we see in it a good likeness of the man. The University of Texas library has a replica of this bust done in bronzed plaster.

Weil
1936

349 Broadway, New York City, where the
photographer, Frederickx, had his studio.
He made the finest portrait of Houston
Collection of the New York Historical Society.

FREDERICKS STUDIO, NEW YORK CITY

THE TRIP that Houston made to New York in 1815-1816, to have his wounds treated after the battle of Tohopeka, was probably his first visit to the metropolis, but he was destined to make many other trips to this great city during his life. Concerning some of those trips we have considerable information; we know something of their purpose and of their results, but Houston made many other trips of which we know nothing. Nor do we know the homes he visited or the business houses in which he transacted the affairs that had drawn him to the city. We do know, however, that he made the Barnum Hotel his headquarters on one of his trips, and concerning this visit to the city there is a brief sketch in this series. We know also that Houston was a personal friend of Charles D. Fredericks, a celebrated photographer of New York, and that this artist made a very fine photograph of the general. Some think it is the best likeness of him extant.

The picture that is presented in this sketch is of Fredericks' studio at 349 Broadway. It was in this studio that Houston sat for the famous Fredericks picture.

Old Baylor Female College, Independence, Texas, to which Sam Houston brought his daughters, Nannie and Maggie in the fifties. The dormitory is at the right. Collection of Baylor University, Waco

BAYLOR FEMALE COLLEGE, INDEPENDENCE, TEXAS

THE PUBLIC school system of Texas was not set up until 1854, and then it was three decades before it came to be a flourishing institution. In fact, it was well into the 90's before it could begin to hold its own with the parochial schools, or those established by private capital and taught, or controlled, by the owners of the institution. Therefore, the larger, and usually the better, schools during the early days were those established by the different churches. Of these church institutions one of the earliest to be organized was Baylor College at Independence. As organized in 1845, this institution was divided into two departments—the Baylor Male College, and the Baylor Female College. By an amendment made to the constitution in 1867, the Baylor Female College became an integral institution with its own board of trustees, but it remained located at Independence until 1886, when it was moved to Belton. In 1925, by another amendment to the constitution, the name was changed to Baylor College for Women. About three years ago its name was changed to Baylor-Hardin College in honor of wealthy patrons who had made the institution rich donations. It has not lacked a large enrollment of young women from wealthy families, nor has it neglected their needs from an educational point of view, but it has also made it possible for girls from poor families and from homes of moderate means to secure as substantial and as thorough training as their wealthy friends. This has been made possible by donations from wealthy and public-spirited persons, but more especially by the inauguration of a plan whereby needy girls are given an opportunity to pay their expenses by their own labor while they are at school. All Texans should honor and be proud of Baylor College for Women.

It has already been stated that one of the Houston residences was located at Independence. It was on the same street as Baylor Female College and just a few blocks nearer the business part of town. Excepting the home at Huntsville the family loved this home better than any other, and after General Houston's death it became the permanent family residence. When the two older Houston girls were still very small, General

Houston enrolled them as pupils of the Baylor Female College. Whenever the family was staying at Independence, the girls were "day pupils," meaning that they lived at home with the family and attended the college; but when the family was staying elsewhere, the Houston girls became inmates of the college dormitory.

Baylor Female College was a pet institution with both Mrs. Houston and her mother, Mrs. Lea. Both gave a great deal of time and energy to the promotion of the interests of the institution, and both donated as much money as could be spared from their own homes for the outfitting of the dormitory. There is a tradition that tells that Mrs. Lea would, each summer, organize a band of workers who would dry enough fruit to supply the table at the girls' dormitory throughout the school year.

Baylor Male College, Independence, Texas. It
can well be assumed that General Houston was
a visitor at times.

Collection of Col Andrew Jackson Houston La Porte, Tex.

Wall
1935

BAYLOR MALE COLLEGE, INDEPENDENCE, TEXAS

HOUSTON'S interest in the education of his sons was deep and practical. In the spring of 1863 he came to feel and know that his time on earth was limited; so he made his will. Concerning the education of his sons he left this admonition to his wife: "My will is that my sons shall receive useful and solid education, and that no portion of their time may be devoted to the study of abstract sciences. I greatly desire that they shall possess a *thorough knowledge* of the English language, and a *good* knowledge of the Latin language. I also request that they be instructed in the knowledge of the Holy Scriptures; and next to these that they may be rendered thorough in a knowledge of Geography and History. I wish my sons early taught an utter contempt for novels and all light reading. Above all that pertains to my sons, I wish particular regard paid to their morals, as well as to the character and morals of those with whom they may be associated, or by whom they may be instructed."

We have no record that Houston ever visited the Baylor Male College at Independence, but it seems a safe assumption to believe that he did. As has been said in a previous sketch, this school was chartered in 1845; in 1886 it was moved to Waco and re-established under the name of Baylor University. It is the largest Baptist institution in the Southwest. Mrs. Houston, who was a devout Baptist, wishing to execute her husband's will to the smallest detail, considered that Baylor Male College was the place in which her sons might develop the most desirable morals, while they were acquiring a thorough knowledge of the English and Latin languages and of the other branches of learning that their father had specified for their education. We have records to show that all of them except Sam Jr., were trained in this institution.

William M. Rice - Cherry home, Houston.
Sam Houston was often a guest here.
Collection of Col. A. J. Houston, La Porte

Cherry House, the Home of William Marsh Rice

WHILE at Cedar Point in the summer of 1861, Houston fell victim to a malignant fever. For many weeks his family and friends despaired of his recovery. During the period of his convalescence he was despondent; he was lonely for old associations and old friends. Houston, the town named for him, was not far away. There he had many friends, as well as many enemies. There had been enacted his political triumphs during the early years of the Texas Republic, and Houston never ceased to love the place. One of the old-time friends who still lived in the town was William Marsh Rice. Hearing of Houston's illness, he went to see him and carried him back for a long visit in his Houston home. The change did the general a great deal of good, and by the late fall he was enjoying robust health again. During the next year Houston was a frequent visitor in the Rice home.

William Marsh Rice and his heirs have left enduring monuments to their name at Houston, Texas, in the magnificent institution of learning, Rice Institute, and the imposing pile of masonry known as the Rice Hotel. This great hostelry stands on the site of the early Texas capitol and is a majestic reminder of the rapid progress that has been made in the city within a hundred years. Notwithstanding these enduring monuments to the Rice name, the old family mansion was falling into decay, when the beauty of its architecture appealed to the taste of a woman artist. She bought "Cherry House," moved it out of the din and dust of the business center, and created out of it one of the most interesting art studios in Texas. Its exquisite panelings might well be the envy of a prince's mansion.

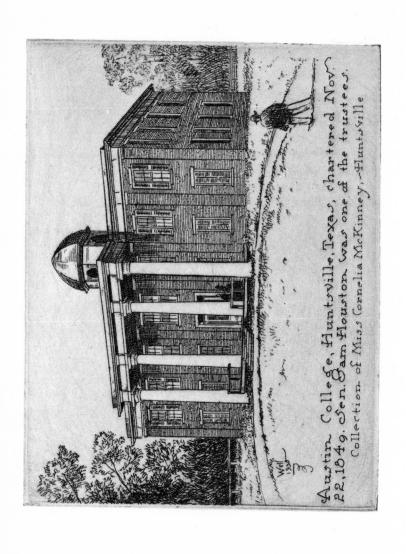

Austin College, Huntsville, Texas, chartered Nov. 22, 1849. Gen. Sam Houston was one of the trustees. Collection of Miss Cornelia McKinney, Huntsville

N THE late fall of 1861, the Houstons moved to their Independence home, but the general was restless there. He himself said that his "thoughts and yearnings turned to Huntsville." In this little town he had spent some of the happiest days of his life, and there were many ties of a personal nature that beckoned him back to the place. One of the minor interests of his life in which he had taken the keenest pleasure was his trusteeship of a small institution of learning that had been established in Huntsville in 1850. This school was Austin College, and it had been established by the Presbyterian church.

The Presbyterian church was not one of the pioneer denominations in Texas. Although there were a good number of people scattered throughout the colonies who had been communicants of that faith before leaving their homes in the United States, they had never had a church organization in Texas before 1838. At that time a church of twenty-two members was established. Ten years later this denomination had a membership of five hundred souls who composed thirty-two church organizations, governed by three presbyteries and administered to by eighteen ministers. At the organization of the first presbytery (1840), that body had discussed the matter of establishing a church school, but they were too poor to do more than talk about it. But the talk and the work to that end went on for ten years, and in 1849 the question was definitely settled by making a final decision on the place for its location and on the method of raising the necessary funds for the setting up of the school.

The school was established under Reverend Samuel McKinney as the first president, in a one-story house thirty-five by sixty feet in area. By the next year, however, the school had grown so that a larger building had to be provided. A sum of $10,000 was raised, and a contract was let for the construction of a two-story brick building to be erected on a five acre tract that had been donated in the south part of the little town of Huntsville. Specification was made that the building must be finished by the last Monday of July, 1851. June 24, 1850, was a gala day at Huntsville; it was the day for the laying of the corner stone of Austin College. Tradition says that Houston laid the corner stone during a pelting rain while the Reverend Samuel McKinney held an umbrella over his bared head, but the college annals do not verify this tradition. A program of the occasion is to be found in the college archives, and it shows that the ceremonies of the day were in the hands of the Masonic Order. There was much marching and speechmaking, but for the ceremony itself the program shows that the Reverend R. E. B. Baylor gave the invocation; Grand Master Neal of the Masonic Order laid the corner stone; and the Reverend McKinney made the speech of the occasion. Sam Houston is listed as one of the most generous contributors to the $10,000 foundation fund, and as a member of the first board of trustees. a position he proudly held to the day of his death.

Houston took a great deal of interest in his office of trustee of the college, as well as in every other matter that concerned the institution. The strong man had a warm sentiment for this struggling Presbyterian school, for in serving it he always felt that he was paying a tribute of respect and love to the one woman who throughout the years had remained the heroine of his life—his mother.

Austin College remained located at Huntsville from 1850 to 1876, when it was moved to Sherman, and there it is still operating as the senior college of the Presbyterian church in Texas. Its old building at Huntsville became the property of Sam Houston Normal College, and today it stands, minus its cupola, on the grounds of that institution now known as Sam Houston State Teachers College.

"Steamboat House," Huntsville, Texas, where General Sam Houston died, July 26, 1863. The room in which Houston breathed his last is the lower west bed-room marked with arrow. Designed by Bernhardt Wall

THE STEAMBOAT HOUSE, HOUSTON'S LAST HOME

WHEN Houston's longing for his old friends and neighbors at Huntsville determined him to return to that town in the late fall of 1861, he tried to buy again the old home that he had sold a few years before, but the owner would not sell the place. Houston was determined, however, to return to Huntsville; so he rented a newly built house in which no one had ever lived. Some imaginative person had dubbed it the "steamboat house" because of a fancied resemblance between it and a river steamboat. Indeed it was a queerly constructed building, and Houston was never particularly fond of it. But it did not take Mrs. Houston and her mother long to make a homelike place of the new abode, and the family was soon happily situated and contented.

They sorely missed the presence of the eldest son in the new home, for Sam, Jr., was far away in the Confederate army. His mother and his sisters were ever busy knitting garments or making something for the boy's comfort, in the hope that there might be some way to send a package to him. General Houston watched the papers and investigated every report that came from the war zone. As is always the case when a member of the family is at the front in war times, all the Houston household lived in constant dread that the news might come that the young man had been killed or severely wounded; nevertheless, all remained as cheerful and as happy as the seriousness of the times permitted. The old general's eyes sparkled with love and pride whenever young Sam's name was mentioned, for he was inordinately proud of his namesake, and secretly gloried that the fighting spirit of the Houstons had run true in his first-born son.

The rear of the "steamboat house" still stands, but the front part was torn away years ago; so it bears little resemblance today to the home in which the Houstons lived and in which the great hero of Texas died.

Smither-Wynne House, Huntsville, Texas. Erasmus Wynne and Robert Smither were close friends of Houston. Collection of Mrs. I. D. McFarland, Houston, Texas

The Smither-Wynne House, Huntsville

AMONG the Huntsville citizens Houston had always been known as "our neighbor," and once more among his beloved "homefolks," he resumed his old-time habit of taking his early morning walks and of stoping for a brief chat or a cheery word at the homes of his friends. It required only a short walk for him to call on Dr. Banton, Dr. Markham, the Wynnes, and the Smithers. The Smither-Wynne home, where he spent many a social hour, still stands, but it is now a hospital. It is beautifully located on a rolling hill, surrounded by stately trees, an ideal spot in which to restore the weary body and mind to health.

But Houston's days were not all spent in revery, or in reminiscences with old friends over former trials and triumphs. He was still a man of action. He visited the schools, the stores, the courthouse; he began again, in a small way, the life of a husbandman; he watched his flocks of sheep; and from time to time he made a few speeches, if he thought they might alleviate distress or encourage those who were disconsolate. He never lost faith or pride in Texas, and he began to do what he could to engender in the hearts of her distressed people the old patriotic fire, against the time of her Gethsemane of trial that he clearly saw must come. Before the war began, he foresaw the result; he sorrowed for the period of reconstruction which he prophesied much as it came to pass. He also prophesied that Texas would lift itself out of its desolation and become the leader of the nation. And Texas has prospered, but we must wait longer still for the fulfillment of the entire vision.

"Shepherd's Valley", Henderson Yoakum's home, nine
miles from Huntsville, Texas. His "History of Texas"
was written in the upstairs room with the dormer window. Yoakum was Houston's attorney, 1852-54.
Collection of Mrs. I. D. McFarland, Houston, Texas.

HOUSTON missed the association of an intimate friend of earlier days during his last years at Huntsville. This man was Henderson Yoakum, a prosperous lawyer whose home was at Shepherd's Valley, nine miles away. Houston and Yoakum were congenial friends, and while the general was away from his home attending to his duties in Washington, Yoakum always acted as the legal adviser for the family, attended to the absent senator's business affairs, and kept a guarding eye on the Houston family. During these years Yoakum wrote a book, a *History of Texas*, in two volumes, and it has been rumored in Texas that Houston had a hand in the writing of this work. That rumor is probably not true, but there is little doubt that Yoakum had access to many of Houston's private papers, and he is certainly indebted to Houston for the use of many of the public documents that he cites. Modern historical critics have adjudged Yoakum's work the best of all the earlier histories of Texas, and it is still used as a reliable source for the period it covers. It is interesting, however, to read a criticism of the book by an able contemporary. Ashbel Smith said concerning this book—and who of all Yoakum's contemporaries was more competent to judge it than Ashbel Smith?—some very uncomplimentary things. Smith said: "Yoakum's History, you know, I dare say, under what inspiration it was concocted . . . . is hasty, prejudiced, ignorant, compiled without investigation even of the slender resources which might have been collected and taken to Huntsville. It is incorrect, incomplete, false in its statements on important events to a degree that would astonish a person not familiar with the general unreliability of history. It is a burlesque of history, hardly accurate enough for the columns of a daily newspaper." One wonders why Ashbel Smith did not try his hand at writing a history of Texas. He was certainly competent for the task. Since he did not do it, Texans will have to continue being grateful to Yoakum for the work he left, imperfect as it may be.

Shepherd's Valley is still standing, and is in about the same state of preservation as is shown in the picture. But our picture does not do the place justice. The artist has not shown —indeed he could not, if he gave a good view of the house—the beautiful trees, the sloping green hills, the shadowy valleys that make a view of startling beauty. Indeed, the location of Shepherd's Valley is beautiful enough to inspire even a plodder to do good work.

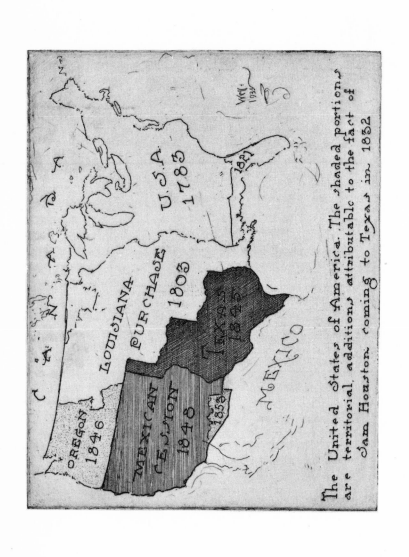

The United States of America. The shaded portions are territorial additions attributable to the fact of Sam Houston coming to Texas in 1832

The Map of the United States

O N RAINY days, or when the sun shone too hot for an aging man to venture out, Houston read his newspapers, Shakespeare, the Bible, Congressional Reports, or the latest war news. There was another document frequently seen in his hands, a map of the United States that was divided into sections, showing how territorial expansion had taken place from time to time. The records of history show that each imperial acquisition, after the establishment of the original thirteen colonies as a nation, might be attributed to the influence of a single man, either through his power as a government agent, or through his political maneuverings. Indeed, it might be said, looking at the subject from one point of view, that it was George Washington who won the independence of the thirteen colonies and made their union as a nation secure. The Louisiana Purchase is generally attributed to Thomas Jefferson. After that, all the continental acquisitions, except Alaska, may be lumped together and attributed directly or indirectly to the intrepid valor, genius, and patriotism of Sam Houston. In the acquisition of Texas, resulting in the Mexican War which, in turn, brought as its result the acquisition of the Mexican territories, Oregon, and the Gadsden Purchase, Sam Houston had a vital part; his influence and his life work are indelibly stamped on the map of the United States with respect to the West and the Southwest.

These facts partly explain why Houston loved to fondle this map; why his eyes brightened and a smile played over his countenance as he traced along some of the lines, and why a sigh, or a tear, came when the boundary of the disrupted Union was reviewed.

Sam Houston's Grave, Huntsville, Texas. His epitaph reads:: The World Will Take Care Of Houston's Fame. ~ Andrew Jackson.

SAM HOUSTON'S GRAVE

IN midsummer of 1863 it became evident to those who watched that the sands of Houston's life were running low, and that no champion would be strong enough to come "in time" to snatch him from the clutches of man's eternal foe—Death. Sam Houston, to whom Texas owes so much, the man who gave to her unstintedly of his talents, his tissue, his time, his very life, the man whose last breath was the word "Texas," died on July 26, and was borne from the "Steamboat House" to the graveyard, only a few yards away, where he was laid to rest during a rain-storm that sobbed and moaned a requiem for the dead. Out in the nation that he had loved so well civil strife was raging at its height. Brother was slaying brother; and few knew, or cared, that Sam Houston was no more. So, a simple slab with its simpler inscription marked his grave. But, later, when animosities had passed away, when an intelligent people had come to understand more thoroughly the man's true worth, when they began to realize the great work that he had wrought for Texas, they gratefully reared a monument of fine proportions at the head of the simple slab. The great sculptor Pompeo Coppini designed the stone, but Houston's old chieftain and beloved friend, Andrew Jackson, long years before had phrased his epitaph: *"The World Will Take Care of Houston's Fame."*

A List of Sources for the Historical Sketches

I. Manuscripts.

    1. *The Sam Houston Papers*, University of Texas Library. (This is a collection of Houston materials now being assembled by Dr. Eugene C. Barker, Head Professor of the History Department of the University of Texas. There are at present more than 4,000 documents in this collection.)

    2. *The Ashbel Smith Papers*, University of Texas Library.

    3. *Frank Brown's Annals of Travis County*, University of Texas.

    4. Records of the Travis County Clerk's Office.

    5. Various letters from persons concerning buildings or other objects represented by the pictures.

II. Newspapers.

    1. *Arkansas Gazette*, various dates.

    2. *Arkansas Advocate*, various dates.

    3. *Austin City Gazette*, various dates.

    4. *Dallas News*, various dates.

    5. *Galveston News*, various dates.

    6. *Telegraph and Texas Register*, various dates.

    7. *Texas City Gazette*, various dates.

III. Books and Periodicals.

    1. *Authentic Memoir* (published anonymously but is the acknowledged work of C. Edwards Lester) 1855.

    2. Brown, John Henry, *History of Texas*, 2 vols., 1893.

    3. Foreman, Grant, *Pioneer Days in the Early Southwest*, 1926.
        The Advancing Frontier, 1933.
        Indian Removal, 1932.

    4. Garrison, George P., *Diplomatic Correspondence of the Republic of Texas*, American Historical Association Record, 1907.

    5. Guild, Jos. C., *Old Times in Tennessee*, 1878.

6. James, Marquis, *The Raven*, 1929.

7. Lester, Charles Edwards, *Sam Houston and His Republic*, 1846.

8. Mayo, Robert, *Political Sketches of Eight Years in Washington*, 1839.

9. Williams, Alfred M., *Sam Houston and the War of Independence in Texas*, 1893.

10. Wooten, Dudley G., (editor) *A Comprehensive History of Texas*, 2 vols., 1898.

11. Yoakum, Henderson, *History of Texas*, 2 vols., 1855.